The Color Lab

Color Cues for Rug Hooking

by Wanda Kerr

Presented by

RUG HOOKING

Copyright © 2018 by Ampry Publishing LLC
Published by
AMPRY PUBLISHING LLC
3400 Dundee Road, Suite 220
Northbrook, IL 60062
www.amprycp.com

www.rughookingmagazine.com

All rights reserved, including the right to reproduce this book or portions thereof in any form or by any means, electronic or mechanical, including photocopying, recording, or by any information storage and retrieval system, without permission in writing from the publisher. All inquiries should be addressed to Rug Hooking Magazine, 3400 Dundee Road, Suite 220, Northbrook, IL 60062

Printed in the United States of America
10 9 8 7 6 5 4 3 2 1

Photography by Wanda Kerr
On the Cover: *The Light Catcher*, designed and hooked by Wanda Kerr, 2017.
Food photography by Prime Publishing
Cataloging-in-Publication Data
Library of Congress Control Number: 2017961619

ISBN 978-1-945550-27-0

CONTENTS

Introduction 1

1. What is Color? 4

2. Hue, Color Families, and the Color Wheel 8

3. Value 22

4. Saturation 42

5. Temperature 54

6. It's all Relative: Color Planning 64

7. Creating Contrast 74

8. Creating Transitions 86

9. Creating Glow 98

10. Creating Depth 108

11. Color Q&A 112

12. Color Creativity 122

Conclusion 129

References 130

The Light Catcher, 14" x 28", #8-cut hand dyed wool. Designed and hooked by Wanda Kerr for her Spin a Line series, 2017.

INTRODUCTION

I don't know if you are the kind of person who reads introductions, but I sure hope you read this one, because it will help you use this book to inspire deeper learning: the kind that is from the heart, not the head—a true understanding.

For years, I've encouraged rug hookers to embrace color through dyeing and design. Of course, gorgeous dyed wool begs an exquisitely designed pattern to play with, and the reverse is also true. One process kindles the other. They are two parts of a circle that round and flow from one to the other. It is a joy-filled process that can help us explore and reveal ourselves, to uncloak our artistry.

Most of my published work about color has been about the dye pots—clear, concise directions for dyeing results in splendid wool. But a question would arise occasionally when talking with students: "This wool is beautiful, but how could I hook it? What use is it? How can I apply this to my hooking?"

The first time I heard this question, I was shocked. I thought everyone understood that any wool can be used for anything, if you use your imagination. I had to really think about this—it seemed we had a disconnect. We didn't understand what we had in our hot little hands, and more fundamentally, how it could be used. We couldn't embrace color as the most beautiful of tools that can work as a hammer or a feather, as chocolate or lemon, as a toddler or a ballerina . . . Color is so versatile, yet we don't understand it well enough to communicate effectively with it. We don't comprehend it. It is the deepest of mysteries, though through our process of hooking we sometimes stumble upon a clue. This book is meant to help you work with color more deliberately and confidently rather than waiting for a clue from your creativity detective.

Playing and working with color is one of the greatest pleasures we are afforded as human beings. Color ignites, and it calms; color fills us with joy. It peppers our language and reveals our souls. I've never had so much fun with any set of ideas before. It is the reason I sew, spin, hook, and dye. The permission to play with "everything color" fills me with a delicious zest for life. We revel in color every day—especially as handcrafters who dye their own "paint colors." It is a fabulous vehicle for storytelling and self-expression.

Remember that you are unique, so no one else has your unique way of seeing color—and that makes your contribution an important one. No one else is playing with color as you might. You are about to set out on a journey of knowing and using color more effectively, passionately, and deliberately; to look and go beyond expected outcomes in your work. You will find that color planning comes quite naturally to you once you've learned more about color basics.

Many books explain the science of color: what is it, how we perceive it, how nature displays it, and mankind's thoughts throughout history on the subject. This book is not one of them. I don't want to waste a second of your time or the space in this book to roll around in readings already available.

If I know one thing, it is this: the study of color is lifelong. It is also sequential: one understanding only leads to the need to grasp the next. It will deepen the mystery of color. As this happens, you will develop a firmer grasp on its handle and swing it more liberally and with gusto. Your part in this process is to relax, to be open to what you read here, to process and explore what we will do in this book together. Please lay aside disbelief and long-held, often non-functioning beliefs about color to embrace new views of yourself and your color use.

Introduction | 1

I'm not a color theorist. I deal in realities. You won't hear me talking about primaries, triads, harmonies, and which colors should go together. I also don't get hung up on the imagined non-workable theories. I want to show you another way of thinking. This book is designed to be as simple as possible to help you use color with strength and purpose in your handwork. I want to give you tools to help you overcome problems every color user faces. I will encourage you to stretch your notions and long-held beliefs about color; I aim to understand your difficulties with color and try to ease them.

I'm building you a workbook, a joy book, a solution-to-your-color-problems book. Most of all, I'm creating a place where you can learn more about what rug hooking is all about: color.

Once you grasp the concept of pulling a loop, you are done learning to hook. Yes, you can learn all manner of devices: turning a loop sideways, pulling it high or low, creating fancy stitches, using fancy fabrics, cutting the loops, and on and on. But when all is said and done, a loop has one primary job—to carry the information of color to the viewer. If we ignore that one job of the loops among all the devices, techniques, or tidy loop-pulling, if we focus on all these other things and let color lose its supremacy, our creations suffer. The loop is not more important than the color it is made of.

When I first started rug hooking, I was already interested in color. I had strong likes and dislikes; I had preferred combinations. From the time I was a child, I was told I had a great eye for color. In fact, I really had no idea. Not one at all. Not one idea about what color is, how it acts, what its functions are, or what even makes a color what it is.

When I started teaching rug hooking, I could toss around a few color terms, but I felt unsure and unsteady. I had to refer to notes. I was saying all the correct words in the right order, but I knew I was a windbag. I knew in my heart I didn't have a firm grip on the subject. I had head knowledge of the use and function of color, but not heart-and-soul knowledge, and my work did not match my weak words. My products did not show color craft.

I don't like feeling unsure or confused, so I set about to learn what I could so I could speak on matters of color with all my being, without pre-planning, thinking, notes, or bulky theories. I wanted color to be a part of me. I wanted to speak about it and use it as comfortably as if it were my own right hand.

If spending money means you've learned something, my color-book–buying habit granted me a PhD long ago. It wasn't until I read two or three particular books carefully that I had some "eureka" moments and made some heart connections to color knowing. I've made a list of my inspirational books; look for them on the References page.

I hope this book will stir you to peer a little deeper for greater understanding of the rug hooker's primary tool . . . color.

HOW THIS BOOK WORKS

I've noticed that it is not enough to just read about something. We need to act, to do it. Each chapter contains three sections: information and suggestions to cement that information by doing, further study by reading or looking, and action in the lab exercises.

We will also check in with my friend, Julie Cheeseman, who has been studying color with me for 10 years. She worked independently as she learned, so I have faith you can, too. We will see how Julie reached beyond what she could grasp into the unknown field of color play to get a strong handle on her artwork. Today she is a keen colorist, and that's the highest compliment I can pay a rug hooker.

I'll show you some of Julie's early work.

We will also look at some of my work to illustrate each chapter's instruction. I will recap my main points in the final section of each chapter, which I call "Things to Hanker After."

These chapters are in a deliberate sequence. (It is good to read this book as though it were a novel; the plot of color must be allowed to thicken!) Chapters are built upon those that come before. But unlike a mystery novel, reading the last page won't provide the solution.

If you cannot ken what I'm talking about at any point, don't worry. This is a study book, one to return to time and time again to deepen and enrich your understanding with each reading. Be kind to yourself; the confusion you might feel is only the first stage to a deeper mastery of color. Try doing a lab exercise from the chapter that befuddles you; you might learn more easily by doing. I urge you to try at least one exercise from each chapter. Even if you feel you have already arrived at that peak of understanding color, there are many sides to any mountain or valley.

Julia with her SMALL CHANGE.

HAPPINESS, 39" x 26", #6- and 7-cut wool on burlap. Designer unknown. Hooked by Julie Cheeseman, Meaford, Ontario, 2000–2001. Of HAPPINESS, Julie said, "I still love this rug, perhaps because the saying is so true for me. But looking at it today, I'd certainly change many value-blending sections."

FLOWERS, 30" x 23", #8-cut wool on burlap. Designer unknown. Hooked by Julie Cheeseman, Meaford, Ontario, 2007.

HERON RUG, 25" x 38", #4- to 7-cut wool on linen. Designed and hooked by Julie Cheeseman, Meaford, Ontario, 2014–2016. HERON is one of her recent rugs. Julie's study of color allowed her to express herself in any way she chose. The design was from a photo Julie took in her backyard in Florida.

Introduction | 3

1. WHAT IS COLOR?

The most important thing we need to know about color is this: every color is made up of four important components. We will come back to these four parts time and time again. Knowing them is our handiest tool. These four things are all present at once, in every color we see. The four components are: hue, value, saturation, and temperature. For instance, one color can be yellow, light, bright, and warm. Let's explore this idea.

HUE

Every color we see has a hue, or belongs to a color family, like blue, or red, or yellow-green, or red-violet. The names of these colors are derived from the color wheel. The color wheel is the way we organize hues: this organization smooths out the communication problems we all have when talking about color. It looks like this image on the right:

The color wheel has 12 main colors, though we could have a color wheel made up of 256 colors, or 10,000 colors. I like to keep things simple; when I refer to a color wheel in this book, I mean a 12-color wheel.

Every color we see belongs in one of these 12 color-wheel hues. (Please note this does not include white or black or the shades of gray between them. These are considered to have no color.) The color wheel usually has very bright colors.

To decide what hue or color family a color belongs to, nestle it among those you think it fits with. It will snuggle in if it belongs; if it doesn't belong, it will stand out.

VALUE

Every color we see has a value, its level of lightness or darkness. Of all the tools related to color use in rug hooking or any visual art, value is the most important. It creates form and brings three-dimensional qualities to an object; it is what makes an object look round in paintings and in life; and it allows things to sit in space. We use it to create glow and shine. It allows us to blend or contrast.

Value is what is being described in this common saying from rug hooking: "All rugs must contain light and bright, dull and dark." Light and dark belong together as a concept; they describe value.

Value is measured in steps running from pure white to deepest black. Each step or number of this scale is doubled in darkness from the one before. We use a numerical system for designating this series of value steps, which is known as the value scale.

This sample has a paper-white value on the left, so it is invisible because of its surrounding. This is our first lesson on value!

1 2 3 4 5 6 7 8 9 10 11

4 | *The Color Lab*

There is some variety in the way experts divide up the area between light and dark. In our rug hooking tradition, we think of light and dark but don't expand our thinking all the way to white and black. I have found that using white and black in my work gives it more power and depth. I'm a woman of extremes and love the oomph that using white and black gives my work.

I've divided the values in the previous diagram into 9 parts, plus black and pure white. Value scale tools at artist supply stores can have 9 to 12 values. We could divide the value gradation from white to black into 15 or 25 or even 100 steps, but it is important to note that our eyes best register the differences between 9 to 12 values. If we cannot discern the difference between more than 12 values, it certainly won't be visible to others looking at our work.

We usually dye natural or white wool—we call that value 1. (Adding even a little dye to these wools will pop them into value 2.) We sometimes need pure white to create shine, a sense of wetness, drew drops, or reflections. I often look for man-made fibers like nylon or chenille to achieve stark bright white in my work.

When you need to know which value a color is (and that should be examined pretty much all the time when making color planning choices), there are excellent tools at your disposal. We'll cover all the wonderful options in Chapter 3.

SATURATION, AKA INTENSITY

Every color has a saturation level. This part of color is a subtle tool. It creates a sense of depth; it has the power to make foregrounds rise up to meet us and backgrounds recede into the distance. It makes an element appear solid or wispy, have hard or soft edges. It is what we use to create sheer curtains and scrims, mountains, and magical effects like shine or dust.

Saturation uses a scale and is measured in percentages. One hundred percent saturation means a color is full of itself. We can see this on the left of the diagram. It is filled with 100 percent color; no gray is present. On the right side of this scale is zero percent saturation; this saturation level is devoid of any color and is only gray. Midway between these two points, we have a middle ground of neither bright nor dull. We can see the effects of close up desaturation; the scale literally fades out on the right and seems to be receding.

What Is Color?

TEMPERATURE

There are two sides to the color wheel; one is warm and the other is cool. Blue is the coolest color, and orange is the warmest color. The colors on either side of blue will be slightly warmer, while those on either side of orange will be slightly cooler.

There are two boundary colors, red-violet and yellow-green. You can see them in the middle of this chart. Although they contain parts of both sides of temperature, they are far from neutralized; as a matter of fact, they seem to have become more emboldened and will act as double-strength warm colors. They rarely behave politely in a rug; they can be quite the show-offs.

Temperature is used to add to the value and saturation message. Warm colors draw forward, while cool colors recede.

Colors Are

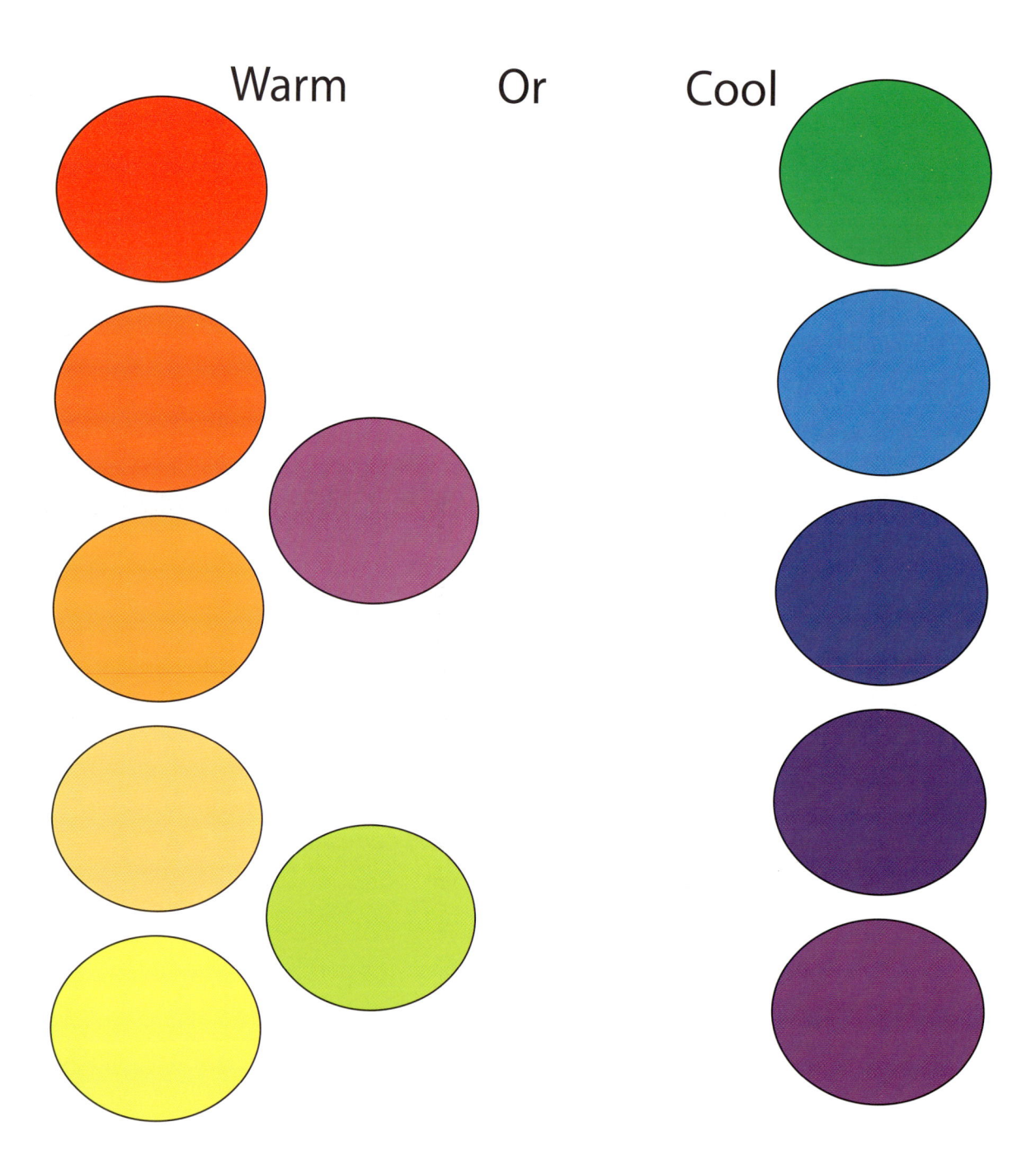

Warm   Or   Cool

6 | *The Color Lab*

THE WHOLE ENCHILADA

Remember when I told you how these four components all happen at once in every color we see? Color is a bit like you or me, with different parts that make us whole.

How are we like colors?

- Value is akin to our body; it is the three-dimensional form maker.

- Temperature is akin to our emotions; they run hot and cold, or they might just be middling.

- Saturation is like our intellect. It is smart and bright, or dull and stupid, or somewhere in between.

- Hue reminds me of our soul. It is who we are; it is where we belong; it is our sense of self. It is what people first respond to in us.

All of these things—body, emotions, intellect, and soul—work together to be us. The same is true for color. Its hue, value, saturation, and temperature create what it is in totality; it tells us who this color is, what it is, and how it might act. When we recognize these parts, we can use it deliberately to create effects we dream of in our mind's eye.

If this representation of color is too abstract for you, we can also relate the components of color to our addresses. An address defines our geographical location, our place on the planet. It tells a lot about us.

- Our surname is like hue. It tells what family we belong to.

- We have a house number. This is like value, it tells where we sit on the light to dark street.

- We have a town we live in, it might be Dullsville or Saturated City. This relates to saturation.

- Then we have a state or province. It might be a warm or cool place to visit.

We are living in all these places, or descriptors, at once. So it is with color: it takes many pieces of information to describe it, to find its home.

LAB WORK

Rug hooking strengthens our color muscles as we develop projects.

Pay more attention to color. Go outside frequently. Observe more slowly, take very close looks at fine details of color around you in nature. When my husband and I are out and see something amazing, The Man is quick to glance and move on. But I always feel the pull of staying longer, looking more closely, bringing in my other senses to hear, smell, and breathe deeply. It is important for my color memory to really be present.

Don't discount man-made color combinations, there is plenty to glean from these, too.

Start looking carefully at color to recognize its four components. Look at the colors you love, like, and hate. Did you know that the colors we love are beautifully enhanced by the colors we dislike? Test this by laying out colors you love and interspersing small amounts of colors you dislike. Almost miraculously they both change for the better.

THINGS TO HANKER AFTER

- Understand that every single color we see has four components to it.

- Recognize that these measurable parts are happening all at once.

- Seek out, examine, recognize, and understand these parts.

2. HUE, COLOR FAMILIES, AND THE COLOR WHEEL

I work with colors to fill up my tank. My love of color fuels my creativity like nothing else. There is so much we adore about hue; it might even be the main reason we hook rugs—to play with the colors we love.

Hue as a word is synonymous with color. They are the same thing. It is first thing we notice about objects: something is green or blue, orange or red-violet, gloriously purple or sunset yellow. Is there anything better to look at than an array of colors?

Of all the parts of color, this one, the color we see (the surname of the color family, I like to call it), is the least important when it comes to practical color use. I know this is terrible news! Unfortunately for us, we fall in love with hue: we see hue first, and we are taken with this first impression, so much so that it blinds us to the higher functions of the color.

In our creative processes, most of the problems we ponder over involve color. The mastery of color can feel elusive, and even after 20 years of serious study, I know there is so much I don't know. I've only scratched the surface.

Don't let that dismay you, my friend; we are starting out on a wonderful journey together and I know the way well. I love a good, deep mystery, and solving color quandaries brings a lot of joy to my life.

When we look at just the four key aspects of color—hue, value, saturation, and temperature—color study becomes a simpler concept.

Remember: color needs to be recognized as an individual, just like a human! It needs some classifying and categorizing. There are millions of colors, and as soon as we develop a system of our own for handling them, they become our pawns. They just wait to do our bidding.

THE COLOR WHEEL

The best way to understand anything is to organize it. Colors have been studied and categorized by scientists and artists throughout history. These various modes of organization have developed into the common practice of using a color wheel to present the full array of colors.

If you love color, you will have seen a color wheel before. You might have seen one in a class, online, in another artist's work, or in displays such as spools of thread, yarn, or wool for sale. Organizing goods for sale according to the color wheel is a favorite way for retailers to set up displays. This is because we are naturally drawn to color arrayed this way. The rainbow spectrum makes our hearts beat faster; it's love at first sight.

The color wheel is an organized display of color families. Each color, yellow for instance, is used on the wheel to represent the greater collection of members of that yellow family. Because each color family has many members, a color wheel can be represented in many ways; we will take a gander at that in a minute. We usually see wheels that use bright colors, like the one here.

A color wheel is a beautiful object to behold. It is made up of 12 colors, each one distinct from its neighbors, yet it runs logically and smoothly from one color to the next.

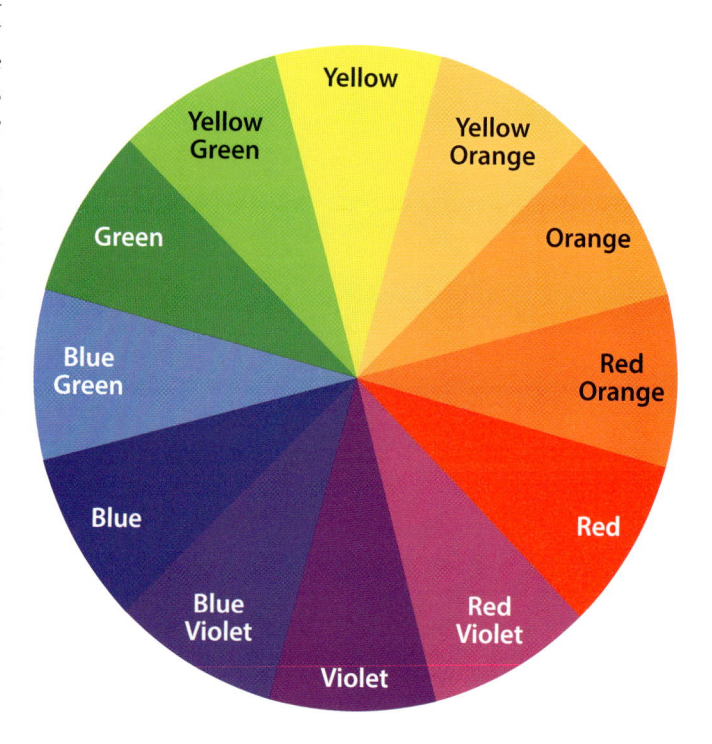

A color wheel has six main colors: yellow, orange, red, violet, blue, and green. Each of these colors has a single name. The other six colors sit between the main colors. They are yellow-orange, red-orange, red-violet, blue-violet, blue-green, and yellow-green. You can see these last six have two names, one for each color on either side of it. These six colors are the transitions between two main colors—it might help to think of them as blends of two main colors.

8 | *The Color Lab*

We often use "fashion" names for colors: brick red, fuchsia, forest green, tiger lily, cerulean, ocean, chocolate brown, olive, burgundy. Even these fancy-named colors fit among the 12 color-wheel families. These colors all have a surname, a color wheel family they belong to. May I introduce you to Olive Yellow-Green or Burgundy Red-Violet?

A color wheel can be arranged with any color at the top. I like mine with yellow at high noon; it's the lightest color, and I like it to rise. I feel balanced by having the darker colors toward the bottom.

Everyone needs a color wheel. Be careful to find a true one. Often displays called "color wheels" are simply color arrays; colors are left out or they don't progress naturally from one to another. Find one that contains true colors that relate properly to one another, that has a natural progression, and that doesn't leave any color out. Find one that shows colors in a balanced way while portraying the truest representation of that color. The color wheel is set up in a natural sequence of colors with a strong presence of each color in its place.

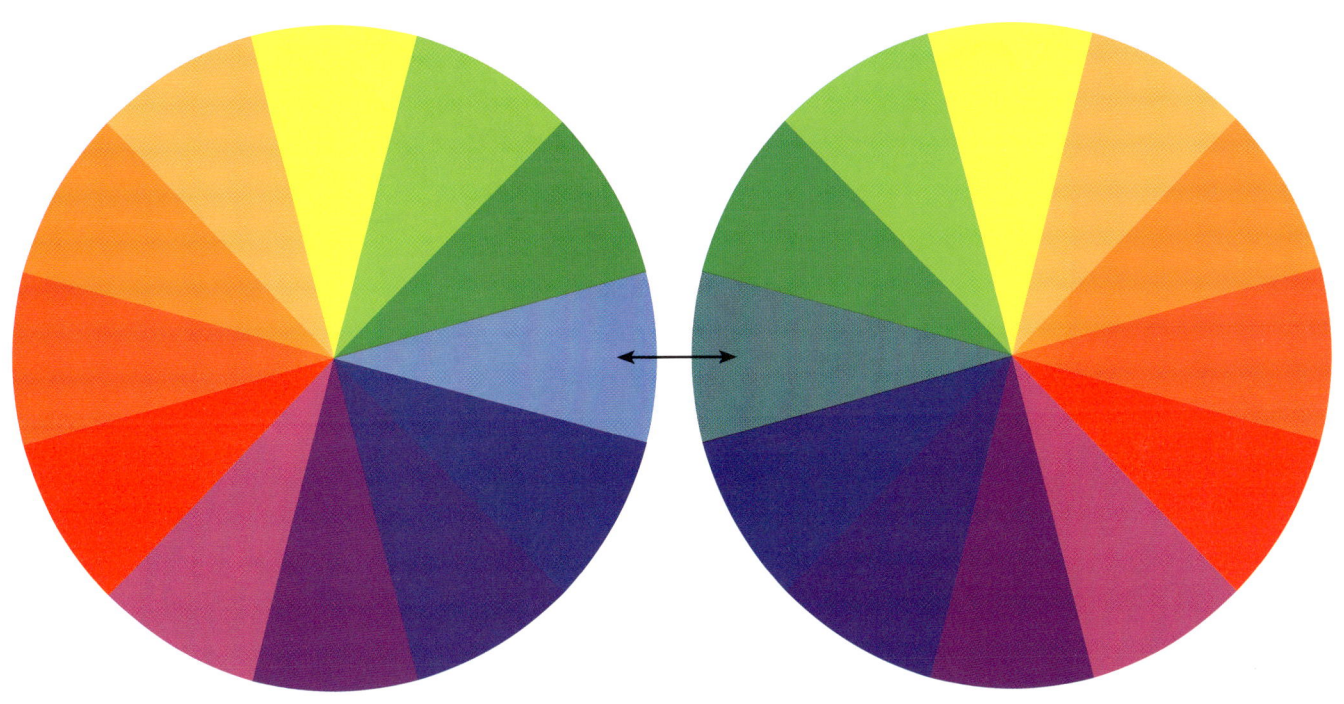

Do you notice how blue-green stands out in this diagram? It is lighter than it ought to be to fit in with the neighbors.

I've created a better blend of green and blue that fits in.

Here the two blue-greens are together; you can judge the differences more effectively.

When you find a good color wheel you have a treasure—a beautiful, reliable, and useful tool for many aspects of rug hooking. Reference a color wheel while dyeing fabric to discern which are opposites, neighbors, and possible wild cards in our formulas. The color wheel helps in color planning a project once we develop our color muscles and can recognize all the ways color-family members can be used.

Hue, Color Families, and the Color Wheel | 9

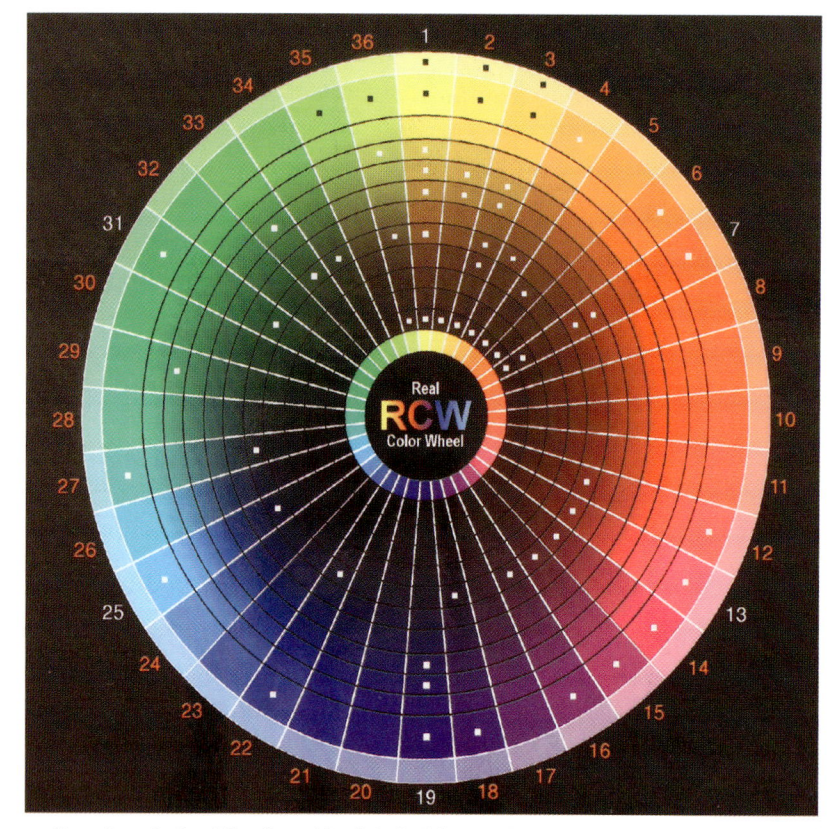

The most correctly colored wheel I've found to date is this one, THE REAL COLOR WHEEL, created by Don Jusko.

You can find this wheel online at *http://www.realcolorwheel.com/colorwheel.htm*. It is composed of 36 colors (this just means more steps are present between our 12 main color-wheel hues). It represents the color-wheel hues in a way that is useful: the colors remain true as they darken and are properly balanced. I highly recommend it.

Joen Wolfrom has a fantastic poster-sized color wheel chart that is a great wall reference, containing 24 colors. She is my colorist hero.
COURTESY OF C&T PUBLISHING

Joen has recently created a smaller, 12-inch version, specifically for carrying around, called *The Color Wheel Companion*.
COURTESY OF C&T PUBLISHING

10 | *The Color Lab*

COLOR FAMILIES

Let's talk more about the color-wheel hues or color family gatherings. You may have experienced this in your own life.

At any reunion, you've got all manner of people present who all belong to the same family. You've got the bright baby, the quiet dull cousin, the darkly handsome older aunt, the intense great-grandfather, the warm-hearted uncle, the sweetly light but dull granny, the wildly strong teenager, the shocking sister, the supportive mother. Our color families are like that: each one has many types of family members.

Yellow, for instance, can reveal many nuances.

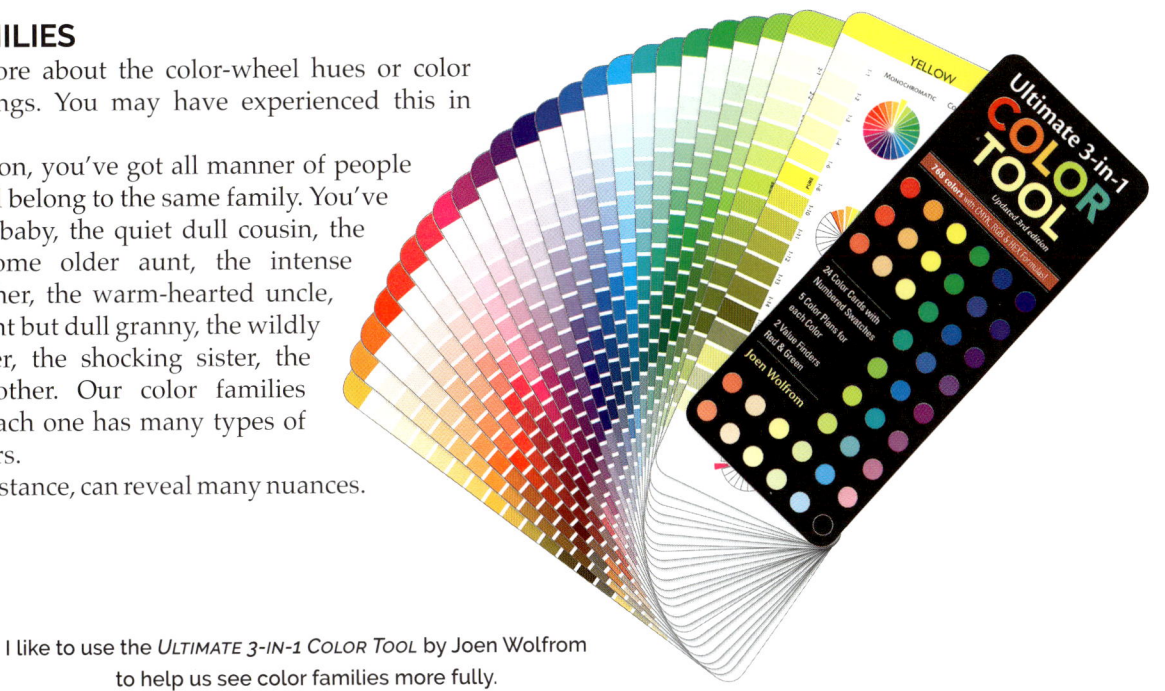

I like to use the ULTIMATE 3-IN-1 COLOR TOOL by Joen Wolfrom to help us see color families more fully.

With the ULTIMATE 3-IN-1 COLOR TOOL, Joen Wolfrom shows us many of the relatives in each color section of the color wheel. It helps us recognize all the members of yellow, from the lightest to the darkest, the dullest to the brightest. Look at the variety below. All are yellow.

Some variations of yellow

Your project might need a yellow that isn't contained in your current idea of what yellow is. You might think of yellow as what you see represented in the color wheel. Yellow might be a color you don't like or cannot use effectively, so you don't explore all it can be.

Yellow can be many things besides what you see on the color wheel. Every color in the color wheel has the same variety of family members as the yellow sample above: all have bright babies, dull uncles, quiet sisters and rambunctious cousins, strong patriarchs and glorious aunts, and they all belong to a single family.

Let's take a closer look. How many family members are possible in each color? Every color on the color wheel will contain lights to darks, bright to dulls, plus warm and cool versions of itself. Wait a minute, I'm about to go in deep here, just for a minute, describing all the ways a family can express itself.

Hue, Color Families, and the Color Wheel | 11

Now back to my gusty dialog for those of you still awake. Remember, all nine values are present in a color family, from almost white to almost black. (Oh, I bet you are saying right now, "Hey, that's not true about yellow." Well, you are right. But that's beside the point right now. Relax a minute and I'll explain that in due course.)

Again, remember all nine values are present in a color family, as light as white, moving through gray, to as dark as black. Now imagine variations of each of these nine values. Each value will have four different combinations: a warm and bright set of each value, a warm and dull set, a cool and bright set, and a cool and dull set. You could also have neutral temperature and neutral saturation in this single value!

(I think I might have sent you running for cover with all that palaver. Remember, if you don't understand something upon first reading it, I suggest you circle or underline it, then come back to it when you are curious or have read further.)

What if we looked more closely and carefully at this, adding a diagram or exercise? Choose a color you like on the color wheel. I love violet, so I'm choosing that one. Let's say we get friendly with violet, value #6. What varieties of saturation and temperature would I see there?

I could have a member of the violet family that is warm and bright, or warm and dull, or I could have a member of the violet family that is cool and bright, or cool and dull—all fitting within that value.

Look at this rich well of colors, all in one family, in a single value in that family. When we consider that the violet family has eight more values to play with, you see that we are blessed with bounty. That's a lot of variety within each family, and they all belong together in that hue set or color family. Remember that each station around the color wheel has 11 values to offer us. They are just like regular nuclear families, with many diverse children who sometimes look barely related, even if they have the same parents. In this case, the parents are a value, the children the variations inside that value.

Technically, some families, like yellow (thanks for waiting, by the way), need a boost from another color to become darker or duller or cooler or warmer. These colors may contain another color in small measures, but you will still know it is a member of its family because it will not fit in any other family comfortably. It will stand out.

Violet color family, and the many value #6 variations in it.

12 | *The Color Lab*

COLOR WHEEL VARIATION

Color use is like music—you can play the same notes in different keys. The color wheel itself can look different than the bright, fully saturated one we usually see. These variations still have 12 colors present, each one distinct from its neighbors, running logically and smoothly from one color to the next.

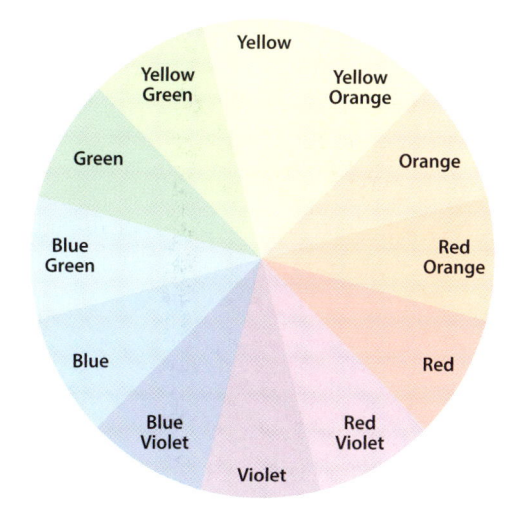

A color wheel can be a collection of colors that are light.

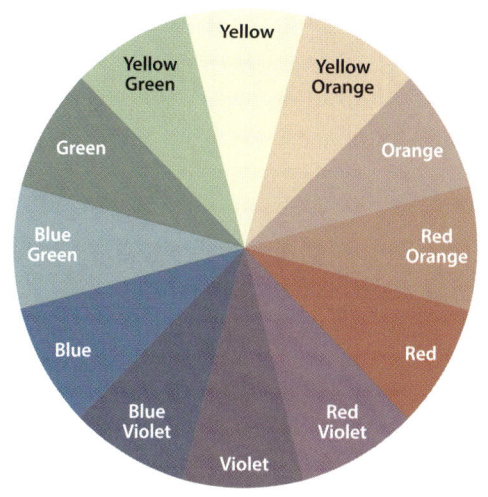

A color wheel can be a collection of colors that are dull.

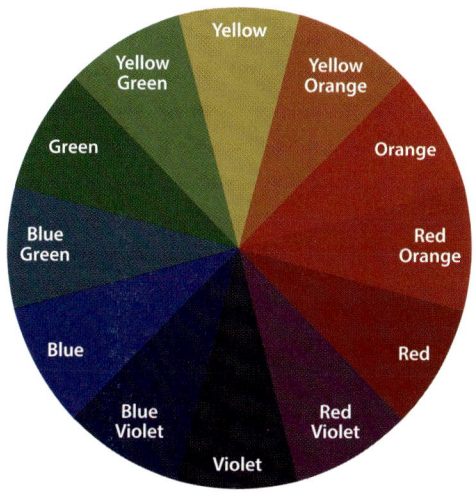

A color wheel can be a collection of colors that are dark.

Think of a summer garden color wheel, an old masters' color wheel, a beach color wheel. Which members of the hue families will you place in each section of the wheel that represents the '60s, for instance? Picking a color theme this way will help you pick colors for your rug's color plan. This is a key component of picking a palette: the theme will inform you of possible colors; it will act as a reference when you need to solve a problem or introduce a new color.

NEUTRALS

While we're discussing hue, I guess we better drag this out from under the bed. It's all covered in wool dust, because it's a bit of a sticky issue.

Mostly we think of neutrals as lacking in color. They don't have a color where they belong on the color wheel. This means black, white, and grays. These are the colors with no color present on the color wheel.

Some people want to include cream, beige, or brown (some earthy colors) in the neutral family. But these examples do have a color—they are made from colors on the color wheel.

Cream can be orange- or yellow-based. Browns are reds, oranges, or yellows, or the colors between these three. They already have families!

When thinking about neutrals, I want to be inclusive rather than exclusive. If some members of the color wheel can make a neutral, why can't they all?

Do you need convincing? Consider this:

In rug hooking, using a neutral can save a bold rug. Most everything we make needs a little neutral zone thrown in. But most often it isn't black, white, or gray we choose. We choose something that has some color leaning to it.

I'm going to go even further and say in any given color plan, a neutral could be anything. We would be fools to suggest neutral grays or brown are the perfect solution for every rug. We need to look at what might act as a neutral among the colors we've chosen.

We must expand our thinking to become more artistic and creative. If it is all right to conclude browns are neutrals, why not dull violets and olives (yellow-greens), or dull oranges and blues?

Why not? Give it a try. There is nothing to lose and much to gain by thinking in new ways.

Hue, Color Families, and the Color Wheel

MY EXPERIENCE WITH HUE

When I first started hooking, I only wanted to use colors I liked. Why not? This seemed right; pulling all those loops took a lot of time, so can't I at the very least be looking at some pretty colors? I think that was okay; I had a lot to think about learning to pull even loops and learning fine shading. About two months and three rugs in, I could see I had a tendency toward blue and away from orange. Now this is no surprise to me, because I have seen that same polarization time and time again. Most of the people I've worked with in my career have the same syndrome. They will love one color but revile its opposite.

If we don't address this leaning in ourselves, we will make pretty uniform creations. There will be no spark, no joyful excitement. They might be middle-of-the-road "decorator" pieces, no different than something we might buy that is mass produced.

When I started teaching, I had to work with all kinds of color themes. I strongly wanted people to use the colors that sparked them. I had designed and made clothes for a living, and I know how important color choices are to help clients feel fully themselves.

I needed wool to supply my rug-hooking students, and even more importantly, I needed to satisfy the rug being made. For instance, if a rug was all blue and cool colors with just a smattering of yellow-green (olive) to warm it up, it didn't quite reach the gorgeousness that throwing a little red-orange (coral) in or a smattering of orange (spiced pumpkin) or some yellow-orange (amber) would bring.

It was through helping my students achieve their goals for great rugs and the exploration for good, better, best solutions for problems in their rugs that really honed my hue awareness. I found sorting my wool and keeping it in color-wheel order helped. I could find the color I needed quickly. This order is also easier on the eye than a riot of jumbled hues in my studio.

I also spent a great deal of time working a paint-by-number website (yes, paint-by-number!). I know that's a dirty catch phrase in hooking, but if you look carefully at any paint-by-number kit, the color use is fantastic. There is depth, there is contrast, and there is color intelligence at work with only nine or so colors. If more colors are needed, you mix new ones from the colors present in the kit. The shapes to fill are excellent, and it is all straightforward. This is the way I think about making portraits: shapes to fill with the right hue. If only we could paint with wool like a paint-by-number kit works!

It was by using Segplay on Segmation.com that I saw how important dull colors were, how pivotal it was to use opposites—lights, darks, warms, and cools—and most importantly, how many colors it can take to render even a single-color object, like an orange. I like looking at where highlights are placed and how shadows are colored and shaped. I nearly fainted with happiness to see the colors at work between these two. I love seeing how a little "do nothing" color becomes the cord that ties everything together. It helped me tremendously to understand that in a great piece of color work, what I like isn't even part of the equation. Perhaps you can find a similar app or program that will let you play in this informative way.

My wool shelves. I store my wool in a very orderly system. I have my wool in hue sections, and then sorted out by value: dark on the bottom, light on top. The top shelf holds my smaller pieces, sorted by value. It's a wonderful filing system that lets me find what I need quickly and soothes my soul every time I see it.

Segplay graphic, a tool I use to help me decipher a color plan.

HOW THE COLOR WHEEL INFORMS US

The color wheel can tell us what color we need as we move from a yellow-green leaf tip into a glorious red-veined center. If we look at yellow-green and we want to move toward red, we echo that movement on the color wheel.

Going toward the right, we would take the shortest route from yellow-green to red, moving through yellow, yellow-orange, orange, and orange-red, to red. It is just natural to do this.

Or we might need to know how to move from a yellow sunrise glimmer to a blue sky. Yes, there will be a brief flirtation with green; this occurs naturally in the sky, too.

Nature reflects movement or transitions from one color to another. It follows the organizing principle of the spectrum that the color wheel is built upon. When we are planning a rug, the color wheel helps us spar up our color choices. We can use it to find opposite colors to place in small amounts, which will pep up our color favorites.

It can help us choose merriment. Say we are hooking a tree trunk. Knowing the position of our main trunk color, say chocolate brown, which belongs in the yellow-orange family, we can use the color wheel to look for "interesting" colors to add in. I could look for an opposite color, like a dull blue-violet or maybe a red brown, while remembering to keep the values close. It might lead me to look at color-tinted grays, which hold a glimmer of all the colors. These additions would be unexpected and hold a whimsical charm, making the work unique.

Understanding where your stash colors fit on the color wheel will help with decision making or problem solving in rug hooking. This knowledge can really enhance your artistry and speed in overcoming roadblocks. You will extrapolate and spin out more possible solutions.

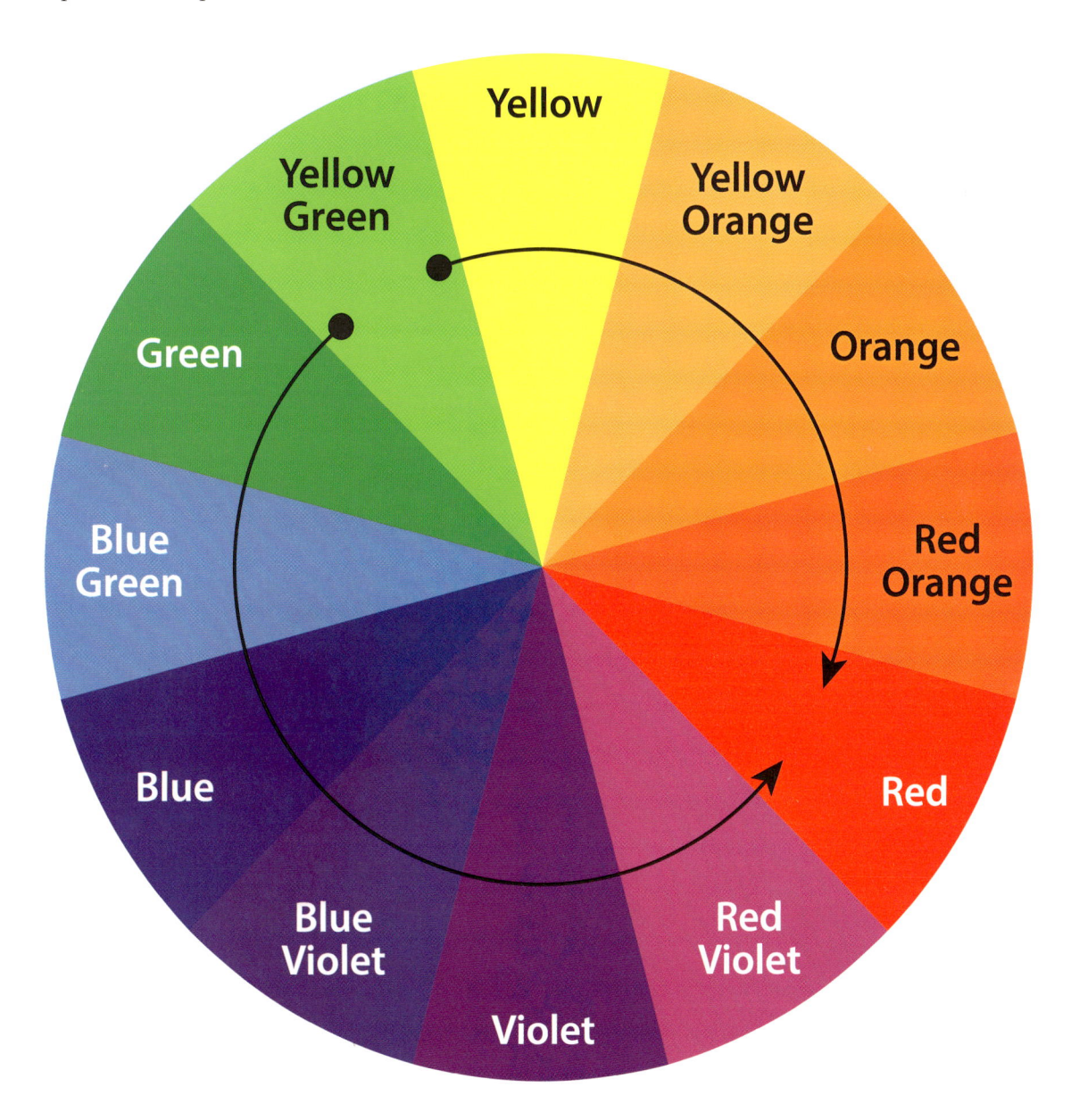

Hue, Color Families, and the Color Wheel | 15

I'm a full-color-wheel user. I don't exclude any color from my palette. I don't care if I like it or not. I pretty much use one or more representatives from all of the colors families of the wheel in some form in most rugs. They all have roles they can play. Using more color will enhance our project, if we use color with understanding. As I like to say, more is more.

Some of my rugs are quietly colored . . . Some are loud!

CEDAR HILL PARK, 23" x 33", hand-torn strips on linen. Designed and hooked by Wanda Kerr, Wiarton, Ontario.

SEPTEMBER, #8-cut wool on linen. Designed and hooked by Wanda Kerr, Wiarton, Ontario.

Some have wonderful color play that can barely be seen but adds merriment overall that is more felt than observed.

Some have scatterings of color that are quite incomprehensible up close. Who knew teeth could cry out for so many colors?

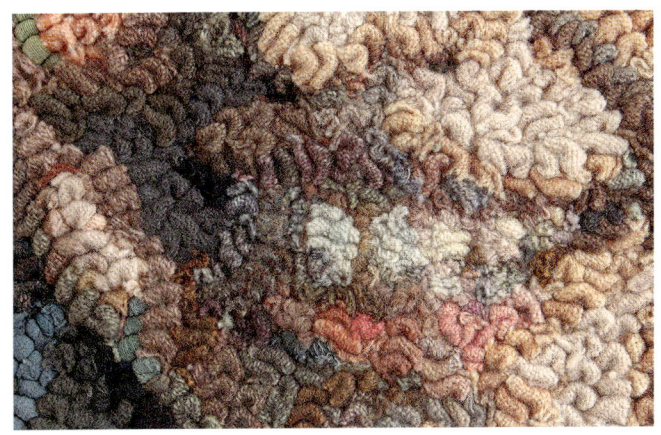

Detail of *Loon by Water*

Detail of *In a Word*

Precious, #12-cut wool, mostly wandered wool on linen. Designed and hooked by Wanda Kerr, Wiarton, Ontario.

Intersections, 24" x 18", #8-cut wool on linen. Designed and hooked by Wanda Kerr during her online class, *Spark*, 2017.

With *Intersections*, I pondered the idea of what happens when two colors meet. What would their potential offspring look like? There is great fun to be had playing with color family match-ups!

In my rug *Precious*, color wheel understanding let me play with my "gray" cat and include olives and violets and blues. It lets flesh be lively with spirit color—you know, the color we feel instead of see? It lets me wander around the color wheel and pick pinch hitters for more traditional, expected colors.

Hue, Color Families, and the Color Wheel | **17**

EXPANDING PALETTES

Many of us like certain colors, and we work easily with them. We know how they will behave with each other. Using our home palette lets us relax into color use. By using this tried-and-true palette, we have pre-resolved any problem we might run into, because we are used to the interactions of this group of colors. This can be very relaxing.

Eventually, we will come to a time when we seek a change, or when what we want to hook can't be delivered with our usual color sets. This can strike terror into our hearts.

It can be hard to slip the noose of our usual output, to recognize our color leanings and tendencies. If we can see color as something we can train to our bidding and begin to feel comfortable going outside our personal, predictable use of it, we can use it more powerfully. We can even flaunt it. Doing the unexpected is risky. We might fail, but it is thrilling, too. (I think some thrills in life are in order once in a while, don't you?) Look for alternatives for your favorite colors by thinking more expansively about other possible family members.

I'm an art-yarn spinner. I started it as a hobby to relax because, well, hooking is my vocation. I needed to have more fun, to find a way to relax. While I spin twist into the wool, I unwind myself. Spinning had a wonderful side effect for me: I was combining unexpected colors that I would not have placed together in hooking. It enriched my color use tenfold. I found a new way to play with color.

LAB WORK

It is very important that you can organize the colors you work with into hues or color families. This includes wool in your stash and dyes in your cupboard. Sorting your wool into color families can really hone this skill. As you begin to sort your wool out and identify where each belongs on the color wheel, Joen Wolfram's ULTIMATE 3-IN-1 COLOR TOOL will help because it shows the great array each of the colors can have in their families.

I have my cut strips organized by color so that I can quickly find a treasure I need. I encourage you to do the same; it will help you do the various tasks I suggest as you create the color work in this book.

Note: Most browns fit into yellow-orange, orange, or orange-red categories.

Look around for color-sorting potential. Hone your hue identification skills wherever you are: Is that pencil really yellow or is it yellow-orange? Is this vitamin red-violet, blue-violet, or violet?

Take a few seconds each day to really look at colors. Ask the question, "Hue are you?" That is so corny, you are sure to remember it.

As colorists, we need good discernment about the colors we see to ken which section of the color wheel it should hang out in, to understand which family it belongs to, and to recognize and sort colors so they are easier to find and use. If you create color order, you won't spend precious hooking time ripping through containers of wool for just the right color.

COLOR PLAY FOR HUE UNDERSTANDING

» **EXERCISE 1**

Sort and store your wool stash according to hue. Sort everything, from the big pieces right down to the worms, into color families. Are you missing some colors? Do you remember I told you the colors you love are enhanced by those you avoid? Get on to fixing this problem as soon as you can. Our work cannot reach its potential, nor can we include magical and unexpected colorations or show some spirited use of color, unless we entertain and court all the colors.

Color family scrapbook

» **EXERCISE 2**

Gather up colored scraps of paper from magazines or paint stores. Choose anything that will glue flat, and include some scraps of your wool. Glue these bits and pieces onto individual journal pages showing members of one color family. Do this with all 12 color-wheel colors for a terrific reference. Not only is this fun, it expands our palette possibilities.

LAB WORK

» **EXERCISE 3**
Create a reference of color themes you like by collecting physical things like cards, pages from magazines, napkins, flowers, or anything that rings your bell. You can collect digital color stories on Pinterest or on Design Seeds (www.design-seeds.com). Practice making color plans with your wool from these sources.

» **EXERCISE 4**
Try making color wheels from things you see around you. My friend Alicia Kay made this amazing color wheel on a walk she took in September.

ALICIA KAY

» **EXCERCISE 5**
Another tool I use is journaling. I start a visual journal from time to time, pasting interesting pages from magazines that provoke me to passion and love. I call them Joy Journals. The only rule is this: I must LOVE them before I collect them. These visuals help me look at and see what color is present in the photo that makes it all work together. That means looking at some pretty ugly colors—at least some that are ugly to me. I still have trouble with peach (yellow-orange)! When I place my visuals into the journal, two kinds of magic transpire. First, I create color connections—joyful relationships between my pictures. To me, these are almost therapeutic to look at. Second, this color journaling also reveals my future color desires, what my eye is loving while my brain is still working in my comfortable color past.

Hue, Color Families, and the Color Wheel | **19**

TOOL MAKING

I think it's high time you dyed samples of your dyes so you know what color they are, as well as their value and saturation. Then you will be knowledgeable about what you are using, and it will help you mix your own formulas and correct them more accurately, too. Imagine baking bread when you can't tell the difference between salt and sugar, flour and oil. Find out what you have hidden in your dye jars.

Take 1/32 yd. of natural wool and dye with 1/32 tsp. of straight dye. You can do this in jars in a dye bath or microwave, or singly in a dye bath in a pan.

Label your samples well. I use the product Tyvek® and a Sharpie® marker to label my wool while dyeing it. (Tyvek is a breathable, insulating house wrap used in construction and for mailer envelopes. It feels like paper and cloth, and it is heat resistant, so it can go through the dyeing process.)

Sort and store your dyes in the same orderly way as you store your wool, by the color wheel. Are you missing a color on the color wheel? If you can't mix it, you should buy it.

Note: Don't get confubbled by dye companies and their fashion names! Look hard at what the colors are, not what they say they are.

I encourage you to explore more colors of dye than you currently use. All acid dyes will work together. There is no reason to stick to one brand if you want some new flavors. Combining dye brands will give you unique colors and expand your stash in new and special ways. Overdye wool you've already dyed with a new color.

THINGS TO HANKER AFTER

As we go through this book we will return to this blue-green swatch in order to analyze it more closely. We will consider its hue, value, saturation, and temperature. In this chapter, we name it: blue-green.

BLUE-GREEN

- Look at colors more closely and carefully and get rid of fashion words in your color vocabulary when talking about color use.

- Know that every color you see has a home at one of the 12 stations of the color wheel, regardless of whether they match printed color wheels, what they have been named, or your idea of what those names mean. Develop the ability to look at any color, like the color on the left, and know what it is.

- Learn to quantify and sort who belongs where, so you can be informed with every one of your future color decisions and speak clearly your color's real family names.

- Encourage yourself to explore outside your usual color choices and use. This might take that piece of wool from the back of the shelf to the top of your "greatest hits" list.

Julie's Work with the Color Wheel

Let's see what Julie has done with the idea of the color wheel. She made a rug in my yearly *Journal Rug* challenge on The Welcome Mat. She let her swirls move naturally, using the idea of hue and traveling around the color wheel.

JC: This was my interpretation of "lines" at the time. I had prepared another whole pattern for the *January Journal*, but it was too restrictive. So, on January 1, 2016, I just started drawing swirls and I felt happy. We were discussing a lot about color on The Welcome Mat, so the idea popped into my head to explore the color wheel in this piece. I LOVED hooking this, and I really like the result. I had no idea how it was going to turn out, which was a new feeling for me.

WK: Julie, what color struggles did you have with this beautiful rug?

JC: The primary (red, blue, yellow) and secondary (green, violet, orange) colors were pretty easy to settle on. Once I got beyond that, I needed to really look at my color wheel—something I had not done before. I had to learn to identify the other colors that I needed within my stash. I wanted the piece to flow from one color to the next—what you call "traveling"—so as to give a smooth transition. I learned a lot about the tertiary (yellow-orange, red-orange, red-violet, blue-violet, blue-green, and yellow-green) colors and soon realized that I just didn't have, or didn't have enough of, some of these colors. My hooking friends came through and all offered me some of their leftover worms to help me fill in. The middle of the rug was a concern as I started, but once I decided to make the colors flow into the middle, it seemed to naturally come along.

WK: What did you like best about working with the color wheel in this way?

JC: I learned where the wool in my stash fit into the color wheel. It helped me realize that I had gaps in my stash of color—not just hue, but value, temperature, and saturation. I learned an incredible amount about color as I hooked: the aspects of color, how to move from one color to another in a pleasing fashion, how to create contrast for interest. I remember saying to myself, "I need dark yellow now, as I move through to orange and to create some contrast with my hooked

Swirls: January Journal 2016 –Mind the Lines. 19" x 31", #4- to 8-cut wool on linen. Designed and hooked by Julie Cheeseman, Meaford, Ontario.

yellows." I couldn't picture what dark yellow looked like, which seemed strange to me. I did some research and found the wool I was looking for in a friend's stash. The same thing happened with yellow-green and blue-green. I took all the greens in my worm pile and sorted by yellow-green and blue-green, a great exercise in itself. Some of my wool was difficult to figure out, so I hooked that wool into my piece where I thought it would go. Sometimes I was right, and sometimes I was wrong. Only by hooking it into my rug did I know for sure if it was in the right place.

Hue, Color Families, and the Color Wheel | 21

3. VALUE

Earlier I introduced you to value. Here is a recap: Every color we see has a value, a level of lightness or darkness. Value has the most important job to do in color. It creates form and brings three dimensions to an object; it is what makes things look round in paintings and in life. Of all the tools related to color use in rug hooking or any visual art, value is the most important one. Value is what is being described in this common saying from rug hooking: All rugs must contain light and bright, dull and dark. Light and dark belong together as a concept; they describe value. Value is measured in steps running from pure white to black. Each step or number of this scale is doubled in darkness from the one before. This series of steps is called a value scale.

This sample has a paper- white value on the left, which is invisible because of its surroundings; this is our first lesson on value!

We use a numerical system for designating this series of value steps, which is known as the value scale. There is some variety in the way experts divide up the area between light and dark.

Every color we see has a value: its level of lightness or darkness.

Value is the most important of all the tools to gather and retain about color use in rug hooking or any visual art. It creates form and allows room for objects and people to sit in space. We use it to create glow and make an object shine; it assists us in blending or contrasting.

It also gives us the ability to use expressive artistic colorations instead of purely realistic ones. For instance, if something is brown in real life, we can use an unexpected color of the same value, temperature, and saturation instead when depicting that object in our art. We might choose olive, dull red-violet, warm gray, or even a dull violet.

Closeup of Lucy in my rug PRECIOUS

My rug PRECIOUS *shows this color pinch-hitting in my Siamese cat. I used all manner of non-typical cat colorations. All the colors worked together.*

22 | *The Color Lab*

Samples of all the colors in *Precious*, arranged according to value.

Look at this study of part of a face. All the values that will be in an entire portrait are in this section. The top example is all as-is textures. The second is using wild, bright colors. One is more successful from a distance than the other because more values are present.

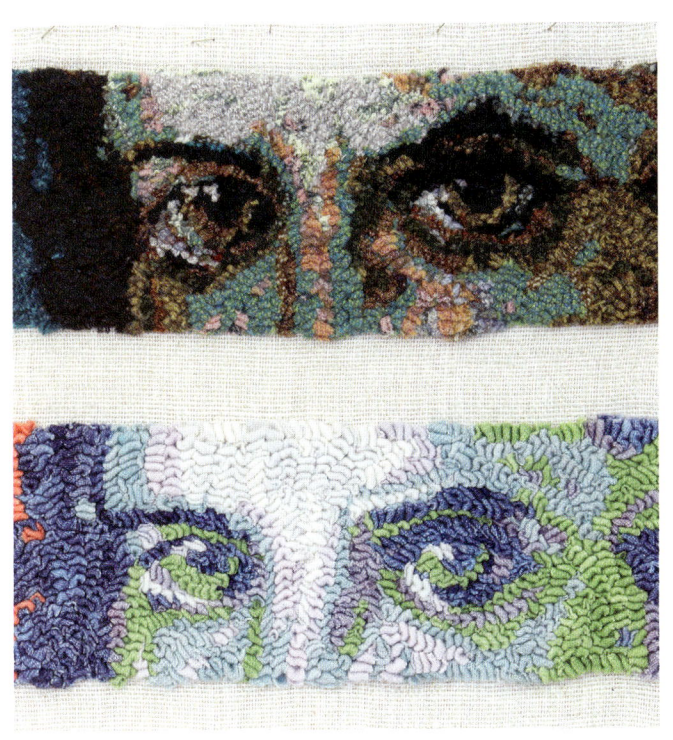

Face slice studies, 17" x 5", #8 cut on top and #12 cut below, on linen. Hooked by Wanda Kerr, Wiarton, Ontario.

Here are the colors I used in the faces. The top row is all off-the-bolt textures. The different values in these colors create the features. Values are making the hills and valleys of the face.

Value | 23

Text and Tweeds

All text has a value.

All text has a value.

All text has a value.

All text has a value.

ALL TEXT HAS A VALUE.

All text has a value.

Text has a value! Text reminds me of plaids; you have darks and lights together, and they make an overall value.

Value in typography is all about the thickness of line, the weight, the space between letters, and the balance and distribution of black and white. We have to look at the whole to determine the value effect. We are used to seeing this, but we rarely pay attention to it.

This value-in-text exercise reminds me of the tweeds and plaids we use in hooking. Thick lines, thin lines, multi-colors, sometimes with strong contrasts—our textures can be puzzling to peg. Values in plaids and tweeds are best read by hooking up a sample. Optical blending allows us to see how this material will read as a valuc. Once hooked, the value of this sample can be easily read using one of the recommended tools you can find later in this chapter. I use this type of wool whenever possible in my work. I love what textures can do with their multi-colored and speckled effects.

Precious, #12-cut wool, mostly wandered wool on linen. Designed and hooked by Wanda Kerr, Wiarton, Ontario.

24 | *The Color Lab*

Okay, it is time to be more concrete. Let's combine the two ideas we have studied so far and look at hue—our color family—and how it relates to value. Remember our guiding principle: each color has four separate components that are happening all at once.

Let's look at our color wheel arranged in a new way—it won't hurt to break free from the confines of the circle, will it?

Colors Have Value

Here the colors are in rows as we might read them, traveling left to right, starting with red.

Let's remove the color from those color ovals and look at their values. I didn't change their position. It is rather remarkable; we don't always see how dark or light a color is.

It is much easier to reckon who is dark and who is light in this chart when the hue/color is withdrawn. You can see that some of the colors, although bright, are also very light (like yellow) or quite dark (like red and blue-violet).

Some colors are naturally light or dark. Red is a darker color than we might imagine, and yellow is always quite a light one.

We are often told the value scale runs from light to dark, but it really runs from white to black. It is easier to understand and use the full array of values if we think of the extremes: paper white to coal black—yes, that very light and that very dark.

Note: On the value scale, each step toward successively darker values is twice as dark as the previous step. To dye them takes twice as much dye in each step closer to dark.

Value | **25**

Every single color we see has a value that fits in a 9- or 11-step value scale.
Let's look at it again with some random wool colors.

All these colors have a value.

Here are the values judged by using my value chips and my black-and-white camera.
I let the chip hang off the darkest value so you could see it was there. This #8 value is a good example of a value disappearing into the wool color, a dark purple. We can easily get misdirected by looking at hue.

Take a careful look at this. When the value is true to the chip, the gray piece of wool disappears.

Values are more accurately judged by looking at a black-and-white view.

So what do we have here? Is it a series of perfect matches? We can see some wool value chips are showing up a little too much. Of course, our wool is mottled, and this creates a mismatch in some areas, but try to look for overall value, a perception that the bulk of the wool gives you. When you squint and you cannot see where the chips are, you are successful. (This is one time in our life when being judgmental is a great thing!)

When you look at this value set-up, you can see some are not perfect, are not that exact value. We expect this because we do not dye with exact values fitting the value scale in mind. What we aim for is a close blending between the value chip and the wool sample.

26 | *The Color Lab*

THE VALUE IN VALUE

It is difficult for us to see value in a color because we are drawn to and love hue. We want to love what we love, don't we? This romance causes all sorts of visual problems and creative frustrations. It's a terrible conundrum that we love color so much, but we have difficulty recognizing its most pivotal part. I'm a bit prone to exaggeration, I admit, but I know for sure that not understanding value and its work impedes the creation of great rugs—the kind of rugs that will throw open a new door in our predictable world.

Knowing the value of a color is very important. Remember, value creates form. Value makes objects, people, animals, buildings—anything really—seem to be three-dimensional, to appear realistic, to have "bones" or structure, to sit in space, and to have air around it. Strong value contrast allows us to see details at great distances; it keeps edges hard.

When we can read values in colors, we make better judgments about the inevitable fixes that happen all the time with our creations. If you aren't making mistakes, then I believe you aren't creating anything! Mistakes go hand-in-hand with the creative process. There are happy mistakes, where you stumble on a solution or an amazing color combination you savor for the rest of your life. (How did that happen? Why did that work?) Then there are the mistakes that try men's souls, seem impossible to solve, and can reduce us to tears.

For instance, have you ever had the problem where something is not showing up in a rug? We all have, and I bet we have all tried to replace it with a completely different hue only to have the same lack of contrast occur. This is because both wools picked had the same value. That is how hue can keep us from the creation of a great rug. An actor might look good, but does he act well? Don't fall in love with hue, because he is a charlatan. Value will stand by you through darkness and light.

A SWATCH AND THE VALUE SCALE

Traditional shading uses value to create form. Regrettably, the tools we use to shade are short on values. Sometimes, the values don't make the appropriate steps between each other. Remember: the color formula should double with each step toward darkness. I know I've already mentioned this, but it is so important!

Sometimes the swatch set covers only middle values—there are no real lights or real darks in the swatch. For great shading with impact, we need to have an almost white on one end or an almost black. To fully shape an object, we need to consider the whole step-by-step darkening value scale and apply it. We cannot be afraid of the very dark and the very light.

A traditionally dyed swatch.

The wool value chips doing their work of finding values.

Swatch and value chips in black and white

Let's look at another swatch set. This swatch is courting the middle of the value scale. We can see that two lights and two darks are left out. Two swatches read the same value. Anything built using these fence-sitting values will diminish in volume; form will not be as strongly present as it might be if you include more lights and more darks.

If we can grab hold of this one facet of color, the ability to decode values in our wool colors, a whole new world will open up. We will get a fresh vista of a view we have stared at a million times, and a new lease on our color life. Once we can read color values, we can choose any colors to create anything and it will have form, as long as we are keeping true to the values of the inspiration. It allows us to use all parts of color to create whatever we like.

A painterly leaf. You can see the colors moving from medium to light, and also bright to dull, dull to bright, warm to cool. It makes the leaf unique, and as a bonus can use up many of the wool worms you have stashed in bins. All those leftover cut strips are too expensive to throw out; understanding what value can do is important and can be thrifty, when we look at our little bits in new ways.

HOOKERS ARE LACKING VALUES

I would say this issue of value is where we fall short as colorists. We need it for form, as I've discussed, but we also need it for contrast. Value contrast is the strongest form of contrast color offers us.

In this rug, black—true black, Johnny Cash black—was used for my T-shirt, my hair, the ground, and the area behind my hair. I'm inside a tent on a wonderfully sunny day. White was used as the tent side billowed out with the wind and we saw grass and sunshine. White is in my eyeglasses, on a post behind me, on my frame cover's label, and at its edge closest to me; this helps this rug be strong and bold. It brings me forward and creates a sense of air around me.

Knowing about value can also help us blend colors, to use similarly valued colors to create the sense of a single color.

28 | *The Color Lab*

THE TOWN HOOKER, 30" x 40", #12-cut wool, and lesser cuts of wool and nylon as needed on linen. Designed and hooked by Wanda Kerr, Wiarton, Ontario.

Value | 29

Detail of *Going Down the Tubes*. I've used close values to create colorful movement in the dark area.

Detail of *And the Day Came*. I've used close values of wool to create the earth the poppy grows in.

When we use the full value scale in our work, we can create a sense of glow: we can let a moon shine, a candle flicker, a light illuminate, the sun sparkle. Having very light in our work to create glow is not enough. We must include very dark as well.

Detail of *If By Light*. In this close-up, you can see a wonderful blending of many, many similarly valued wools to create the sandy dirt moving toward the water's edge.

Do you see how gloriously the sun sparkles on the water? Now look for the corresponding dark that must be present for the light to shine.

I'm devoted to helping you glow and shine as a rug hooker. We will look at how to do this in a later chapter, once we develop our value-seeing skills.

If By Light, 19" x 34", wool, yarn, and nylon. Designed and hooked by Wanda Kerr, Wiarton, Ontario.

30 | *The Color Lab*

TOOLS FOR SEEING VALUES

Training our eyes to see value does not come naturally; we need assistance. There are many ways to learn how to see value in a hue. When we looked at our color wheel array and removed the hue, it made things a lot easier. So, let's look at ways we can remove hue on the fly while we work.

BEHOLDERS

Ruby Beholders have long been touted as the value assessment cure-all. The truth of Ruby is she needs her sister Emerald to be fully effective. A Ruby Beholder only works to read true values in cool colors: greens, blues, and violets. You need an Emerald Beholder to see the true values in warm colors: red, orange, red-violet, yellow, and yellow-green. So, if you want to try this tool, get both. (Both are part of the ULTIMATE 3-IN-1 COLOR TOOL by Joen Wolfrom.) To use these tools, look through the Ruby or Emerald Beholder to see your wool with no color present—only the values are left to read.

PAPER VALUE SCALE

You can use a paper value finder. Go to my online store for a free download: http://www.wandaworks.ca/store/p61/Color_Lab_Gray_Scale.html

My printout will make four value finders. Print them out on card stock, cut them into four pieces lengthwise, and punch a hole out of the center of each value. To use a value finder, simply lay it down on your wool. Look for the circle where the least color shows through, where a blending with the surrounding paper square occurs. You can also pull a strip loop through the hole to determine value.

You can also buy these scales from any art supply store. (Note: they run their numerical system from 10, the lightest, to 1, the darkest.

CAMERA

A camera is the best tool of all for looking at value. It removes any possibility of being influenced by our own predilections. It does not tell a lie unless the camera lens is flooded with light; that circumstance will change the actual value of the colors you look at individually, but it will not change the value relationships between and among colors. You can use any digital camera, your phone, or iPad; all work equally well.

Set your camera to black-and-white photo or download an app. I use one called **Black and White Camera** *on my iPad. It is important not to use a de-saturator or sepia setting or other tonal, noir, or fashion-type setting that comes with your hand-held devices—they will tell you value lies. Take a photo and turn it into a black-and-white version. Sometimes I still can't believe my eyes when the values are revealed.*

TOOL MAKING: DYED VALUE SCALE TWO WAYS

If a paper value finder doesn't work for you, and you relate better to fabric, dye yourself a wool value scale. Here are the directions for small and larger pieces.

Read through these instructions carefully before starting.

Dyeing A Value Swatch

Gather nine jars and a dye bath pot or two to process them bain-marie style. (Bain-marie style uses jars filled with water and wool in a water bath).

This formula needs 1/8 tsp. of black dye in 2 3/4 cups of water. Add 1/4 cup boiling water and stir to dissolve, then add 2 1/2 cups cool water. In this case, accuracy is important. You need to make sure you have enough dye formula to do your measurements. (You will have 4 tsp. left over at the end of the process.)

Get nine pieces of natural wool. Each piece should measure 1/32 yd.

Here's how to do this:

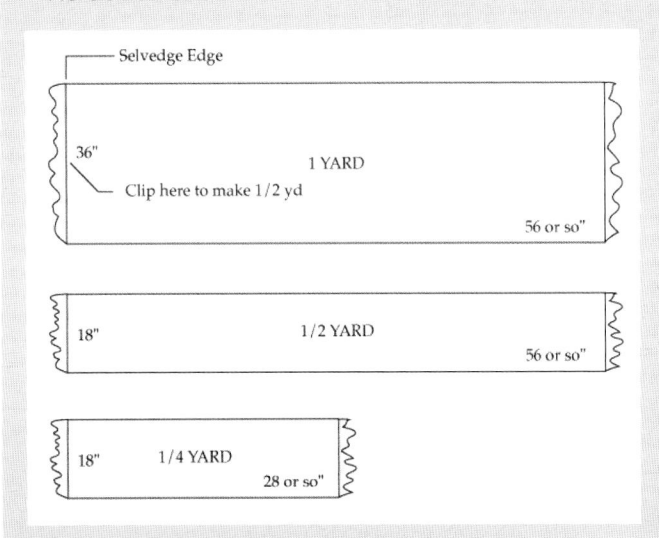

Along the selvedge edge of the wool, cut at 18". Rip it in two.

Fold ½ yd. in half, with selvedge edges together. Clip at the halfway point. Rip it in two. Now you have two ¼ yds.

Each 1/4 yd. contains eight 1/32 yd. pieces, so continue to fold and clip.

Fill nine jars about 3/4 full with water. Make one jar only half full; this will be used for the very darkest value. Put the jars into a dye bath. Add salt, if it is your preference, to the jars.

Soak 10 wool pieces, 1/32 yd. each, until thoroughly wet.

Carefully, and with great concentration, add the following amounts of black dye to the prepared jars. It is best to have no distractions. (It helps to pin signs to each jar with wooden clothes pins. I write directly on the clothes pin with a marker: Jar 1, Jar 2, and so on.)

Measurements per jar:

Note: If you want to use your tablespoon on the last five measurements, look at the amount after the = sign. It will save time, and it is more accurate.

Jar 1: 1/4 tsp.
Jar 2: 1/2 tsp.
Jar 3: 1 tsp.
Jar 4: 2 tsp.
Jar 5: 4 tsp. = 1 Tbsp. +1 tsp.
Jar 6: 8 tsp. = 2 Tbsp. + 2 tsp.
Jar 7: 16 tsp. = 5 Tbsp. + 1 tsp.
Jar 8: 32 tsp. = 10 Tbsp. + 2 tsp.
Jar 9: 64 tsp. = 21 Tbsp. + 1 tsp. (Fill jar half of water)

These directions make you a swatch for your own use.

1. The lightest value will be the undyed piece of natural wool.
2. Add a single piece of wool, one at a time, to each jar.
3. Turn on the heat under the dye bath.
4. Stir the wool in each jar vigorously.
5. Wait for five minutes and stir again.
6. In five more minutes, add acid and stir again.
7. Stir again in another two minutes. This will ensure a smooth swatch.
8. Wait until water clears.
9. Rinse well, dry, and pin together.

I cut strips off the bottom of these and keep the small set in my hooking tool bag. I also add a piece of commercially dyed black for the darkest value, and, of course, leave one piece completely undyed, reminds me of the bright white value #1.

TOOL MAKING: DYED VALUE SCALE TWO WAYS

Dyeing a Larger Set of Value Swatches

If you want to create a bigger value set, here is the best way to do it. I usually dye this one as I feel the measurements are easier to keep accurate because I'm dealing with dry dye powder.

I dye each piece, one at a time, in a dye bath. Make sure your dye is a true black; I used Majic Carpet dyes, but PRO Chem has a good black, too.

For these swatches, use 1/8 yd. pieces of wool. Each line below dyes a single 1/8 yd. of piece of wool.

1/512 tsp. Black

1/256 tsp. Black

1/128 tsp. Black

1/64 tsp. Black

1/32 tsp. Black

1/16 tsp. Black

1/8 tsp. Black

1/4 tsp. Black

1/2 tsp. Black. This makes a wonderful true black.

I add a white piece of wool to the top just as a reference for bright white, though it is the same value as the lightest dyed one.

On a personal note, I've been studying the value scale a long time, and even though my talk has remained the same, my dyed value scales have gotten better and better. I always doubled my amounts, but my refinement toward true black and white have deepened over time. We can't ignore the importance of them or be stymied by what we believe is dark or light. Remember snow white and coal black; don't give Wanda a value attack.

How to Use The Dyed Woolen Value Scale

I like to have a big piece and a smaller piece of my dyed scale to use. I call the little bits chips. I just cut off the end of the swatch or a 2" x 1/2" piece from the larger set. The smaller chips travel around with me in my hooking bag and can easily be thrown down on visual aides to determine value. Sometimes I need to find just the right value for a student's partially hooked rug. When I send the student to my wool, they use the wool chip to find the right value.

Let's pretend you are that student. Lay your value sample down on the wool you want to determine the value of. Stand back and squint a little. When the wool value sample settles right in and doesn't stand out in any way on the wool, then the wool in question is the same value as the value chip. If you are in doubt, try the values on either side of your selected wool chip. It is okay to lay all of them out to determine which are the closest. You will soon see the best match.

I use the larger value swatches for a planning reference. I can plot out values in a rug by laying these swatches down to determine the value contrast I need.

Value plot for a landscape

MY EXPERIENCE WITH VALUE

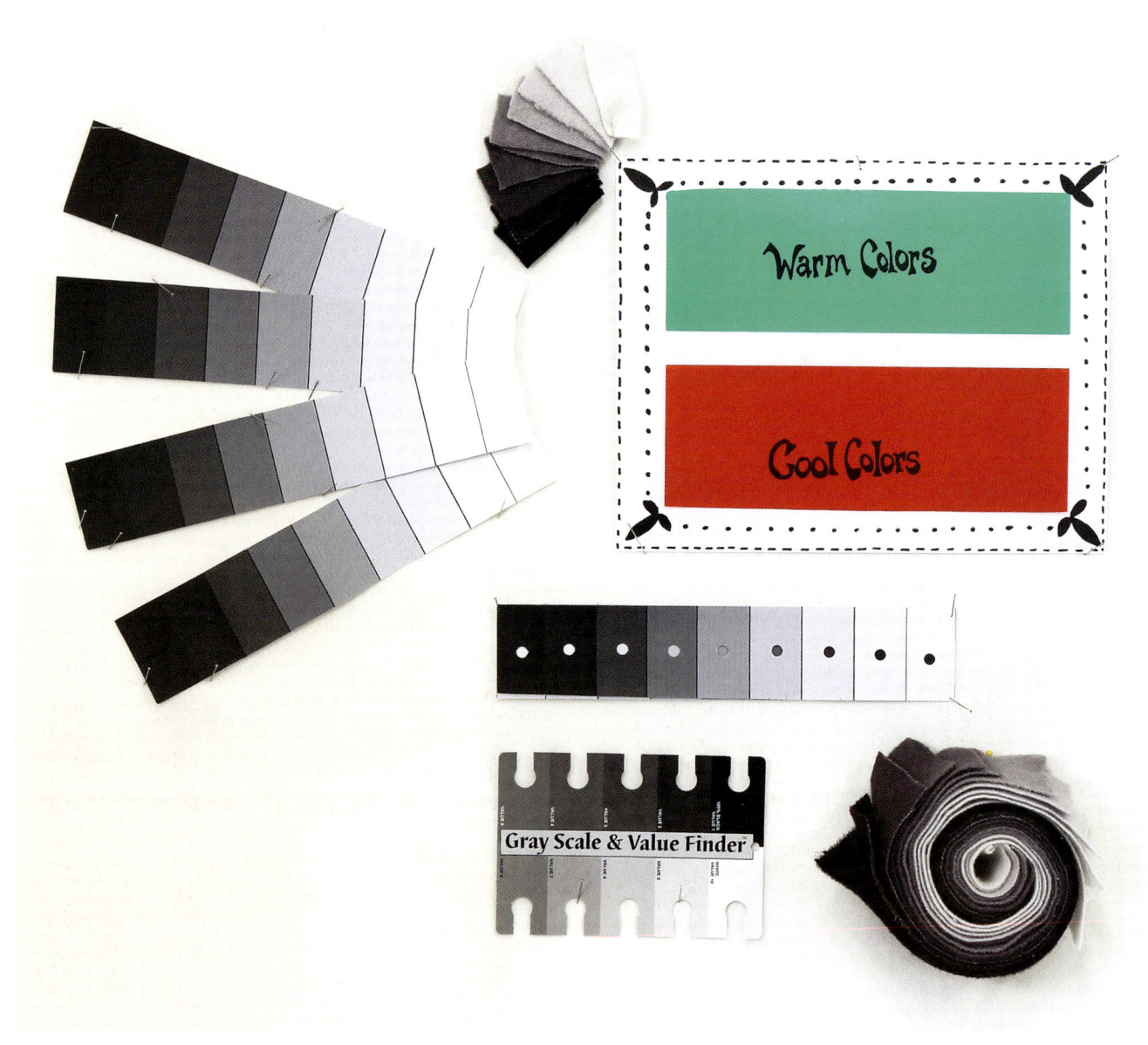

Value tools

When I started hooking, I barely understood I was engaging in color work. I was hooking what I loved; I just hooked with the colors I bought and dyed, and I had on hand only wool colors I loved. I'd say, "I like that color, so I'll hook with it."

One day my rugs were on display at a local arena, and I showed A*BANDON*, a rug that is only a little bigger than the size of a sheet of paper. I also showed a very large rug, M*Y* G*IANT* D*IMPLED* A*RSE*.

While I was making M*Y* G*IANT* D*IMPLED* A*RSE*, people commented on how incredibly bright the colors were. I never once considered they were mostly the same value. I thought their brightness would make a big impact. When these two rugs were hung up on display, the much smaller one showed almost every detail from a long distance away. The big rug barely showed up as anything from a distance. You couldn't tell my arse from the grass.

What a shock that was! It really made me wonder why. Look at the size difference: wouldn't something that big and bright show up well? Why didn't the motifs stand out?

ABANDON, 13" x 17", #3- through 8-cut, wool on linen. Designed and hooked by Wanda Kerr, Wiarton, Ontario.

MY GIANT DIMPLED ARSE, AKA THE CHURCH OF THE HEAVENLY BAWDY, 53" x 58", hand-torn strips on linen. Designed and hooked by Wanda Kerr, Wiarton, Ontario.

Let's look at these two rugs through a value lens.

Hmm . . . that spells it all out, doesn't it? The bright colors in my larger rug just didn't have enough value difference to create any contrast. It was meant to be a colorful salute to a primitive design style. I didn't intend to make such a visual blender. This experience made me really look carefully at my color choices. It prompted me to look more deeply into color. Why was one rug working as an attention getter and the other wasn't?

My brain wanted what it wanted as I hooked MY GIANT DIMPLED ARSE, and it didn't give a toot for the value truth. It just wanted pretty colors. I had to overcome my wants for my work to be more dynamic.

Value | 35

WHICH VALUE CLUB DO YOU BELONG TO?

I've noticed that everyone has a tendency to like one end of the value scale or the other; some only like the middle. We're all card-carrying members of one of these clubs.

| 1 | 2 | 3 | 4 | 5 | 6 |

The Sisters of The Light only like very light and medium values.

| 5 | 6 | 7 | 8 | 9 | 10 | 11 |

The Daughters of Darkness only like dark and medium values and will always lean toward these.

| 4 | 5 | 6 | 7 | 8 | 9 |

Then we have the Fence Sitters, who dislike both dark and light and only desire the middle. That's where *My Arse* was sitting. But generally, I'm a Daughter of Darkness.

To tell which club you belong to, look at your rugs and your wool stash using one of our black-and-white tools. It will soon become clear where you feel most at home. Beware of feeling too comfortable in your safe value club. It is preventing bold choices and expansive color work. It is holding you back from creating the contrast or depth you seek or the glow you wished for when you lit that candle!

Beware of wool shopping and dyeing where you get stuck on a value set and repeatedly buy those again and again, only to have no values available for contrast. Wool gathering should be like grocery shopping: you have to have healthy things and staples as well as all the stuff you love. Otherwise you'd get rickets and scurvy. Don't let your wool stacks be poxed by malnutrition! Go beyond your safe desires.

DISCOVERING YOUR CLUB

Let's find out about you and the wool you have on hand. You will also learn something wonderful to do with leftover cut strips to give them new life and provide vivacity and excitement. This trick is just one of the wonderful things having value knowledge gives us.

We can sort wool we have on hand to create multi-hued same-value motifs or backgrounds. Sorting your wool by value can also create productive order in your wool stash.

Look at the photo of my wool shelves on page 14. At this moment, the colors in my wool stash are sadly depleted. I haven't had time to dye to replace missing colors since I returned home from a wildly successful teaching junket. You will see a lot of jumps and missing values. It is easy to see what the shopping hookers from my class wanted to buy; much of what is gone went to the Fence Sitter's Club.

I have another section I sort by value, kept on the top of my color stacks. They are smaller pieces, only 1/16 or 1/8 yd. It can be hard to see the myriad of colors I have available if they are stacked in a pile. I keep these small pieces sorted by value to create a working stash for myself. It doesn't really matter to me if I run out of a particular wool color. I have many pinch hitters in and around that value that might perform as well—or possibly better! As a bonus, I can quickly grab a single piece to help or demonstrate a new value to a student in a value quandary.

36 | *The Color Lab*

LAB WORK

SORTING EXERCISE

Let's play with some leftover strips, this time looking at their value. This is as easy as sorting laundry, and more fun!

1. Grab a handful of strips and place them on a table where you will have room to work.

2. Pull out all the lightest ones and make a pile. Pull out the darkest ones and make another pile. You will be left with the mediums.

3. Each of these three piles could also be further sorted into light, medium, and dark, if you are working with many colors. (Maybe you won't have nine different values, just like my depleted wool inventory.)

4. Observe what happens as you remove the darks and the lights. Did you notice how lackluster the middle pile began to appear; how taking out those extremes dulled the pile right down to a coma? I hate to be the one to tell you this, but, darling, this is our go-to mode; this is where we all roll to—the middle! We have to stop this horrible condition in its tracks.

5. Compare how well you did by using a value tool. I used the black and white camera app on my tablet.

6. Hook these together to create a reference. I did, and what happens is so beautiful; you can see the worth of these castoffs. Look at this gradient from a distance, and you will see the little vagaries of individual colors disappear and a gorgeous, rich rendering appear. It looks a little like a landscape.

Please make a hooked reference of your own. It is the only way to learn. This trick can carry you to a place of inherent creativity and artistry you've only dreamed of. Every piece of anything you can draw up as a loop becomes as valuable as a hand-dyed swatch.

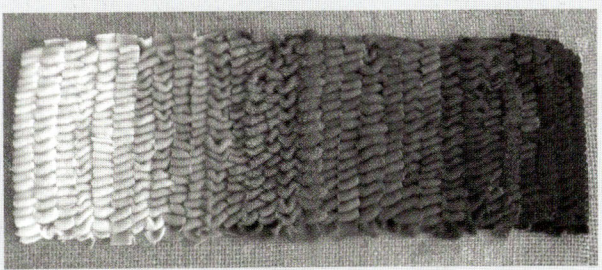

Value | 37

LAB WORK

MORE EXERCISES TO TRY

- Can you create a value scale from variously colored wool? Don't worry about whether they go together, just look for value.

- Examine your stash and rugs to know what values you chose and have a tendency toward.

- Carry around a value scale when you shop for wool. Check off the values you already have plenty of, and look for those you don't have.

TOOL MAKING

DYEING AND VALUES

Dye more values. Try dyeing swatches that double each step and contain very light and very dark. Vary your starting measurement or the strength of your formula. Doubling or dividing by two only changes formulas by one value. When we consider the fact that our rugs are going to fade out over time, it is even more important to exaggerate values.

Every dye formula can become nine values. Most of them are medium valued, so double the amount of dye to move up one value. Cut the amount of dye in half to go down one value.

Exaggerate your values. You need at least a space of two values—preferably three—between colors to create good contrast. Let's make it simple:

- Use more wool or way less dye for lighter values.

- Use less wool or way more dye for dark values.

Go for the gusto. Fight your proclivities!

One of my students once came a very long distance to be mentored in dyeing wool. After a very successful session, she synopsized her experience by saying, "So I must learn to use way more dye and or way less dye." Yes, you've got it! You must move away from the center. We are not lying on an old mattress, my friends; there is no reason to keep rolling to the middle in our work. What looks too bold now will be a mellow beauty as years go by, just like you and me.

THINGS TO HANKER AFTER

- Know that value is the strongest element of color.

- Develop comfortable methods using tools to read values in color.

- Recognize the concept that light and dark belong together as a measure of color.

- Develop the ability to read values with or without tools.

- Actively seek out more values in your work.

Our blue-green is a value #2.

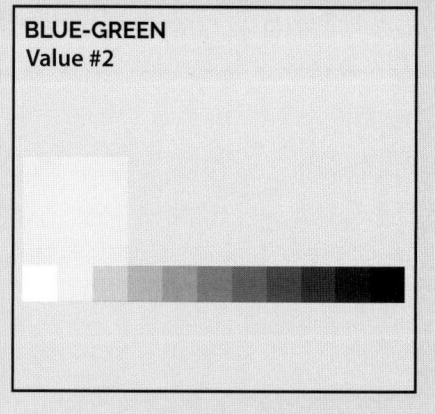

BLUE-GREEN
Value #2

38 | *The Color Lab*

Back in 2010, I gave a little talk on value to my Woolgathering hook-in attendees. I handed out this instruction sheet. Please use it as you like. You can see Julie's rug designed from the patterns on the next page.

OUR STRIPS WANDAWORKS WOOLGATHERING 2010

Our strips. There is no doubt we have them, the question is, what can we do with them? My friend Marilyn Bottjer has so many she has hooked over eight good sized rugs out of them to date, though she swears to me they are mating and raising young in her closet.

You can overdye them, you can hook a hit-or-miss rug. You can replicate anything you want using them! FLOWERS, BIRDS, PEOPLE, SCENES, CREWEL, ORIENTALS . . . anything you see!!!

You have to learn to handle them, to sort them.

You can sort them according to color families . . . that can be useful for using the odd strip here and there. If you want to really go for the gusto while using up your strips, you might want to consider sorting them according to value. Every color has a value, values just don't happen in swatches. The value of a color is part of what makes it what it is; it is a graduated scale running from white to black.

Here is an easy way to sort strips by value. Take a handful of strips and place them before you. Give them a close look. Can you see any darker ones? Pull them out and make a new pile. Are the lighter ones shining out at you? Make a new pile of those. The medium ones will be left.

It is possible to subdivide each value group—light, medium, and dark—into two or three piles using this same system of pulling out the lights and darks. For more excitement and accuracy in your work, you might want to do this when you are working with more strips.

You might encounter a problem with brights: where should they go? They are darker than you think . . . lay them on one of the piles to see if they disappear or get stronger. You want them to fit in or kinda disappear.

Think of sorting your laundry. Have all the loads the same: darks with darks, mediums with mediums, lights with lights.

You will see you probably have many colors together in your piles. The most magical thing about hooking these colors all together as though they were one is the splendid iridescence you can get. Really, it is the only way you can get this effect. You cannot get a true "oil slick" effect by dyeing iridescent wool. The other amazing thing is the speed at which you can use up all manner of business. It won't take long to whittle away your piles of strips when you can hook anything with them.

Sorting them will also help you dye them. Say you have three piles of various colors and you need them all to be dark blue. Make your formula, throw in the lightest ones first, wait a few minutes, then add the mediums, and a few minutes later add the dark. They will all end up being close to each other's value.

See page 124 for the patterns Julie used for her *Woolgathering Challenge* rug.

Julie's Value Work

Julie took up this challenge to create something gorgeous out of her leftover strips. You can see how she played with value and hue and created interesting patches of color inside any certain value shape. These colors work together to create an interesting patina.

JC: I had a lot of leftover strips and was intrigued with this exercise. I soon realized I wanted to combine all the different values to see how the various combinations would look hooked. One square turned into eight squares, and I made it into a mat. Not only did I learn a lot about value, I loved seeing how my 'scraps' worked together.

I wanted to explore value, but this time trying to go from the lightest to the darkest using all the worms that I had (including all hues, values, saturations, and temperatures). I thought out this geometric design, but, again, didn't really know how it was going to work. I made a few modifications to my design in the middle section, just to add a bit of interest. I enjoyed this experience, although I did get a bit bored hooking some sections. I did learn how hard it is to properly place the brights within the "right" value spot.

WK: Julie, what do you find works best to find values in colors?

JC: I follow the process that you taught us in the Woolgathering challenge. I take all my strips, first sort them into light, medium, and dark. Then I sort each pile again into three piles, ending with nine different piles of values that have all different hues, textures, etc. Then I take a black-and-white picture of the individual piles. If a strip is too light or dark, it will stick out in the black-and-white photo. I tweak each pile using the black-and-white photo setting. I still find the brights to be a bit of a challenge. I place them where I feel they will most likely belong. I find often I have to make adjustments with them as I hook along.

WK: Do you think you are a Daughter of Darkness, Sister of the Light, or Fence Sitter?

WOOLGATHERING CHALLENGE, 29" x 19". Mostly #6-cut on burlap. Designed by Wanda Kerr and hooked by Julie Cheeseman, Meaford, Ontario.

40 | The Color Lab

JC: I believe I am a Fence Sitter. As I worked on these rugs with my own stash, it was clear right away that most of my stash was of medium value. I now purposely look for lights and darks when I shop for wool. Although still my eye and brain are pulled toward those mediums!

WK: How has your thinking about value changed from 2001, when you started hooking, to 2010, and now in 2016?

JC: When I started hooking in 2001, I didn't have any concept of the term "value." It was many years later that I started to read about value in color (through The Welcome Mat and other places). The first time I consciously tried to separate my wool into values was during the Woolgathering challenge exercise in 2010. I was amazed at how that worked—all those different colors, within a value pile, could have the same value. I just couldn't believe at the time that I could interchange any of the colors in the one value pile. In 2010, I tended to use only the blues and purples from the various value piles. I didn't feel comfortable at the time using just any color from the "correct" value pile. In 2016, I specifically set out to sort my strips by value again with the intent of hooking a rug using all colors within each value pile. I found the process quite uncomfortable, but when it seemed to work, I kept going. This was an incredible learning exercise.

Value Study: February 2016. 27 1/2" x 15". Leftover worms, varying from #4- to 8-cut on linen. Designed and hooked by Julie Cheeseman, Meaford, Ontario.

4. SATURATION

Every color has a saturation point. Saturation is about bright, dull, and what stands between those poles. It is measured in percentages: 0 percent looks completely dull—in other words, plain gray. On the saturation scale, 0 is the lack of any color. I bet you are thinking, "Isn't the value scale gray too?" Right here I want to step in and save you some befuddlement.

Yes, we also show values in gray, but don't get confused. These two elements of color, value and saturation, are separate things. They both have a component of gray. They both use gray to examine a part of color with no hue present. They are both measures, but they don't measure the same things. For instance: a ruler and a measuring cup both have lines and numbers in common, but they measure different things. We know we can't use a ruler to measure sugar for our cake recipe or use a cup to measure an inch. Gray is like those lines and numbers—it is part of both saturation and value but measures different things with the absence of color.

Here is what a color looks like from 100 percent saturated, aka bright, on the left, to 0 percent saturation, aka dull, on the right.

Here is another. Note this saturation array's color is bright, but it is not as bright as the one above it. It is still this particular color's 100 percent saturation point. If it got any brighter, it would no longer be this particular color. We will talk more about this anomaly in the relativity chapter, so don't worry if this sounds confusing.

Let's combine the ideas of value and saturation and look at our samples in gray scale by taking away the color. This shows us the values in black and white. Here is the blue sample:

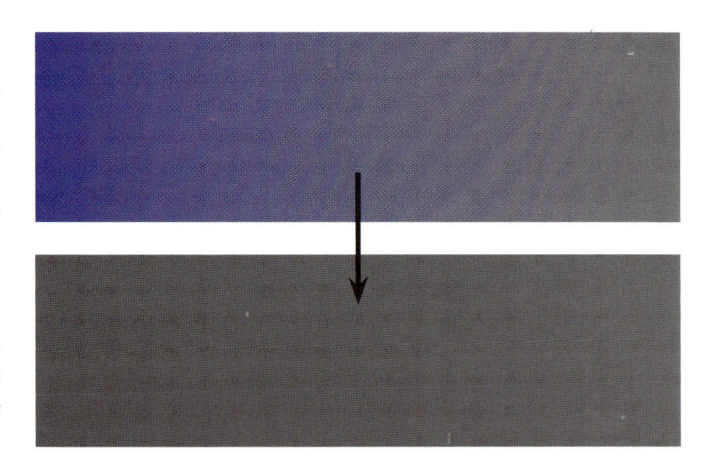

Sometimes this is a shocking revelation! Color can disappear, but the values stay the same or move very little. Let's look at our coral sample.

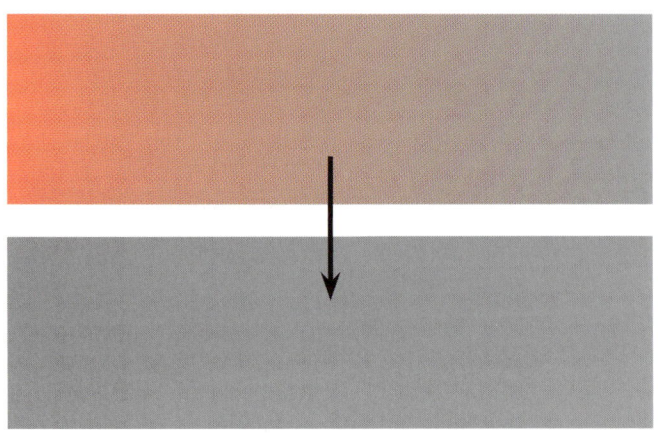

Equally shocking! A color can move from 100 percent saturation to 0 percent saturation and barely move along two points on the value scale. In both these cases, the value remained the same. We cannot rely on saturation alone to create striking effects in our work.

Did you hear that? Saturation alone cannot create strong bones in artwork. Value provides the framework. Luckily, we can use the two things in tandem. Remember, color has four components all working together at one time: hue, value, saturation, and temperature. Color is such a wonderful tool. It makes me so happy to use it!

The Color Lab

Now back to our saturation scale: 100 percent is a complete fullness of color. It is intense. Sometimes saturation is also called intensity. It is color-full.

On the other end of the scale, at 0 percent, only gray is present. No color is available in that percentage.

Here is another way to look at saturation: by 25 percent increments.

| 100 percent saturation | 75 percent saturation | 50 percent saturation | 25 percent saturation | 0 percent saturation |

Saturation scale: 100 percent on the left, 0 percent on the right.

Saturation is the subtlest knife in our color repertoire. It is so delicate and thin we don't notice we've been stabbed until we are well away. It is a quiet one. Most often, it is used with value and temperature to reinforce their important work.

Saturation helps us dim backgrounds to allow shine elsewhere. It makes things move away from the viewer or bring them toward us.

Many artists pay no heed to this concept of creating depth of field. They keep everything on the same plane. They swish merry colors around and, beautiful as they are, they often have similar saturations. Even if the picture is drawn with perspective, something seems incongruent.

Remember this rug with lovely, bright colors but no depth of field? Although an artist might choose to create a flat aspect as their style of art, usually we do not mean to have our work turn out this way.

When flat aspect is a problem, as in this *Giant Arse* rug, we will see things close up and far away using colors with the same or close saturation percentages. We are disquieted by this lack of attention to saturation's finer points. Things that are close to us need to be brighter, darker and/or lighter, to contain strong contrasts, be more warmly colored, and have more details, more contrast, and more visible textures.

Look what happened to me in *My Giant Arse* rug. This rug is suffering in so many ways.

Saturation | 43

Land masses and objects far away are duller and lighter, they lack contrast, have no texture, and are coolly colored. These rules apply to any subject we hook. Yes, of course, landscapes. But also, portraits, where we want the delivery of cheekbones and prominent noses. When we want ears to each appear on their planes, the eyes to be sunk in, the cheek to recede to the ear, saturation is the color tool to use. In geometric projects, we can use it where we want areas to appear to be on top of others.

If an artist misses this saturation boat, it creates a sense of unease in the onlooker. Our eyes tell us something isn't right. Our mind feels confused. It isn't as pleasant to view as it could be. Color has not been used as well as it might be.

MEASURING SATURATION

So how can you be a proper saturation user? First, practice looking for and diagnosing saturation. A saturation tool is not as easily created as a value tool.

Dyed Saturation Scale. I dyed this one entirely by eye, which I know is NO earthly use to you.

It is difficult to produce a dependable, working saturation scale. We will talk more about this later in this chapter. As a fallback, I rely on the idea of a brightly colored T-shirt that is washed so many times it loses all color. The new T-shirt is bright with all its color, but the one that you've washed 200 times might not have any color left at all. This makes a good reference: I ask myself, "How many times has this color been washed?" This is not very concrete, but I hope this mental picture will lead you to the beginning of saturation discernment. We could also use our value scale and ask ourselves, "How close is this color in question to gray?"

There are many online diagrams of saturation available. These might help you get a firmer idea of what various saturations look like. For the best results, search the phrase "saturation scales."

WHAT IS BRIGHT?

We are also mightily influenced by our innate ideas about what bright means.

This might mean bright to me (100 percent saturation).

This might mean bright to you (60 percent saturation).

I often find myself in a contradictory position when talking to people about color. They might comment when looking at a color, "That's very bright." On the saturation scale, it might only be at 75 percent or 60 percent. It is not really bright at all, but to that person and their notions about colors, it is bright indeed—not scientifically bright, but perceived as bright. I suggest politely to them that although they feel that the color appears bright, that is different than what is scientifically bright.

Just as we have a comfort zone of values and hues, we also feel wonderful in certain saturations. We delight in them. We might even revile scalding brights or the ultra dulls. Much of our bright/dull leanings come from our upbringing. Maybe you weren't encouraged to be showy or flashy, to delight in racy colors or be like a chorus girl. "Proper ladies" know the accepted colors to wear and might refrain from including improper colors in their work. This may be a pretty deep-seated proclivity we are not even aware of. I've often been typecast, wrongfully I might add, as having very bright wool.

This is an interesting fact: we might not even notice something dull if brights are present.

MY EXPERIENCE WITH SATURATION

I want to release you from all this excess baggage about saturation. Be free of conforming. Any great artwork will include a variety of saturations. I don't remember exactly when I started to think about saturation. I always knew it was important to balance areas of high saturation with areas of low saturation. If we don't, we run the risk of exhausting our viewers' eyes.

I love hooking landscapes and designing my rugs. HURON ISLANDS was the first time I thought about what I could do to create the illusion of distance in my hooking. I think its exciting possibilities became evident when I attempted to make a horizon appear and be effectively distant.

HURON ISLANDS, 24" x 13", #3- to 8-cut wool on linen. Designed and hooked by Wanda Kerr, Wiarton, Ontario.

I made the non-sun parts of sky duller than the water, and the reflection brighter than the sky. I was feeling my way here in this early rug. I did not know that my loops' true job was to deliver color information.

I tried loop machinations many times in those days to create effects. I now call these "devices." My device in this piece was to use multi-hued #8 strips in the foreground and gradually diminish their size and movement and the number of colors used as I moved toward the horizon line, which is a #3 cut. This device creates a certain "trick" effect and does not succeed in creating depth if viewed from a distance. I imagine now how much better the outcome might have been if a duller saturation had been used as the water moved toward the horizon. Color can make effects appear quickly and easily without manipulating the loops themselves in any way.

CEDAR HILL PARK, 23" x 33", hand-torn wool on linen. Hooked in rows from bottom to top. Designed and hooked by Wanda Kerr, Wiarton, Ontario.

In CEDAR HILL PARK, it's late winter, and there is ice dammed up across the bay. It is a very dim day, but there is still a reflection on the water of the sky and the escarpment. The sky is trying to spin some color out to us, though very dimly. Here's how saturation works in this piece. The near trees are brighter than those duller trees across the water. The water reflects the land mass, an escarpment, in a duller way than the original. You can see there is a brighter, wild patch; this represents something in the water. Using duller colors to portray reflections is not a hard-and-fast rule, so don't take it as such. The sky has similarly valued colors in it, with some much duller and others brighter. The brighter sky colors reflect more dully on the water.

In LOON BY WATER, color is doing a lot of delicate work. Brighter saturation is used to boss up sections of the water, and some open areas are brighter than ice-covered ones. See how my crooked tooth is catching the light, making it brighter than the rest of my teeth? There are bright spots here and there in the ice close to my body. Notice how my down coat and my surroundings are sort of the same color? How do we know where my coat starts and the ice stops? The colors of the ice around my coat are all a little brighter than the coat itself.

See my scarf? See the dull and brighter green creating the sense of pattern in it? Look at the lighter patch of flesh on my sunlit cheek; observe how it is light but duller than the high point of the cheekbone.

Look at the far shore, how dull it is, and now search for the similarity in color family you see in my brighter beret. Saturation is making all of these subtle things appear; it is bringing a sense of reality to the scene.

Maybe you want to look for hue and value when you are looking so close. See how they are working their magic together?

LOON BY WATER, 36" x 23", #12-cut wool and nylon on linen. Designed and hooked by Wanda Kerr, Wiarton, Ontario.

Look at this play of saturation and greens in a detail from my rug, DEARLY BELOVED. The three-lobed leaves are layered, and the one on top is bright and dark and perversely cool. The three-lobed leaves under the top ones are duller and warmer. This temperature reversal defies common thinking. Normally we use warm colors to advance and cool colors to recede. There are other factors at play in this design: the size of the leaves and the use of dark and bright for the larger leaves. The sunlight brings a warm glow from behind the shrub and creates a dark, cool first layer of leaves. Notice the background shrub with small leaves, all lighter and duller and mostly warm, leading to my warm sky.

46 | *The Color Lab*

Let's look at saturation in HIGH PRIESTESS. It is one of my more recent rugs, so I'm a little more sophisticated in my use of this subtle tool. Look at the water's edge; the froth from a recent gust of wind is much lighter and duller than the water itself. Looking up from that spot into the water, you'll note that she is behind a veil. This veil separates her from the greater world, and it is laid over several parts of the scene: the moon, sky, trees, and water. We know the veil is transparent, but we also know it has some effect on the things it covers. Saturation helps create this effect, along with value. Everything behind the veil is lighter and duller than the colors that are outside the veil. This was interesting to work. During the process, I got advice a few times to remove that strange line in the water, because people didn't know what it was building.

Look at the books to see how I varied the saturations of both the pages and the colors of the books. It makes them look worn or new and creates variety. The owl acts as a unifier between the bright light column of the tree and the dark bright ironwork; he is a quiet mediator hooked in mostly dull colors. In her mirror, all color is gone—0 percent saturation. She isn't looking at her colorful self, but is holding the mirror up for you to see yourself. She's letting you add your own intensity.

HIGH PRIESTESS, 24" x 44", #8- and 12-cut wool and yarn on linen. Designed and hooked by Wanda Kerr, Wiarton, Ontario.

Saturation | 47

LAB WORK

If you want to master saturation, you have a little detective work to do. The first step is finding out more about your own saturation proclivities.

- What do you classify as bright? Is it really scientifically bright?

- Can you find brighter colors out in the world than the ones you have in your wool cupboard?

- Do you have dull wool? Is all your wool dull? Or is your wool mostly somewhere in the middle?

- Where do your rugs sit on the saturation scale?

Once you've answered these questions, it is time to play with saturation. I think it would be quite shocking if I suddenly suggest you start using colors that are way out of your comfort zone in your creative work. So, let's play in a safe way: no threat, no cost, no problem.

» **EXERCISE 1**
Go to a store where you can get paint chips. Pick out six colors you love a lot, ones you might date for years, even marry. Ones that make your heart skip a beat. Then pick out six colors you don't like at all, that you really dislike. Horrible, vile colors. Try to resist making a color plan. You can save that fun for another day.

Now arrange all 12 paint chips on a page from bright to dull. Remember value and color/hue have nothing to do with saturation sorting: you are looking for the presence of gray, the washed-out–T-shirt quality. You are looking for the strongly colored, bright, new T-shirt and those T-shirts in the middle of their life, washed quite a bit but still having some color life left in them.

Which make you the happiest? Do you favor one end or the other of this saturation array? Maybe you are a fan of the middle. Whatever it is, this is your saturation safety zone. Now that you have this info, you can start to work around it to bring more variety to your work. Grab a handful of wool strips and line them up from dull (no color) to bright. Then hook this sample up; it can be multi-hued or single-hued.

48 | *The Color Lab*

LAB WORK

» **EXERCISE 2**
Take a gander at your wool stash. Your leftover strips can really tell a clear story too. Can you sort them?

Pick out the brightest first.

Then look for the dullest. Next, sort the remaining colors for brighter and duller.

You will have created piles that look something like this: The brightest colors are on the left, the dullest on the right. Can you hook a gradient from dull to bright with them?

We should aim to have a variety of saturations in our wool. What are you missing? Fill in some of those "holes."

If most of your wool is dull, from the 0 to 30 percent range, start slowly by dyeing or buying yourself some wool that is 45 percent or 50 percent. Don't try racing to 100 percent right away or you'll scare yourself. Go slowly into this new place. If you never have any dulls, do the same thing. If all your wool is 75 percent saturation and up, look to 55 percent or 45 percent saturation for the first steps toward saturation freedom. Once you get used to looking at these "new to you" colors, try adding them to your rugs in small places. I promise it won't hurt at all! Let your rug's colors sing on the mountaintop; these will be a clarion call to the low saturation valleys.

Saturation | 49

LAB WORK

Several photo-inspired landscapes by Wanda Kerr, #2- to 12-cut wool on linen or rug warp.

» EXERCISE 3
Making little landscapes can really help you polish up your saturation chops. They are small, so you need only go beyond your comfort zone for one or two strips. Use a photo and try to stick to its colorations as closely as you can, paying careful attention to value and saturation. Use any cut or materials available to you. Search for the saturations present in your visual aid, then replicate them to give your work depth of field.

TOOL MAKING

SATURATION AND DYEING

I would love to have supplied you with a perfect method to dye a saturation tool. I have failed you in this respect. We cannot predict the ways any two dyes will interact to create a good workable scale for everyone. When I'm dyeing a scale, I often resort to my eye.

Here is one I've dyed with blue and black. My Majic Carpet dyes are not all the same strength. Blue is lighter than black when dyed in the same amount.

I started with 1/8 tsp. of Blue for the 100 percent saturation side and 1/32 tsp. of Black for the 0 percent saturation side. The rest was a pure jazz riff on what I could see in the pan.

You can try this. Remember, the object is to have less color in each subsequent swatch until you reach a completely colorless formula of black or gray.

DE-SATURATION THROUGH OPPOSITE COLORS

When dyeing, it's fun to find opposite colors of equal saturation and use them to cancel each other out to make grays. Remember, opposite colors are those directly across from each other on the color wheel. It works best when you can find two dye colors that are of equal strength and have the same saturation and value using the same measure of dye.

- You will need dyed samples of your dye colors to determine hue, value, saturation, and temperature. This will allow you to evaluate the components of color in each one to determine if you have equally saturated, opposite colors. (If you need instructions, refer to the dyeing segment in the hue chapter.)

- If you don't have opposite dye colors that are equal in value and saturation with the same measurement on hand, that's ok. You can use less of the stronger dye or more of the weaker dye to help them become more equalized.

Bright to dull dyeing sample

The Color Lab

TOOL MAKING

- If you don't want to make gray, you don't need to have dyes of equal strength. The interesting relationship of a dominant color and a weaker one creates beautiful colors. Increase or decrease the measure of either color as you wish. Choose one dye for what I call Formula One, and its opposite for Formula Two. Next try exploring the different color you can produce by switching the positions of the colors—using the opposite color as the lead and the main color as the supporting lady. This is lots of fun and the results are magnificent. Be aware that these transitions are often very close in value, so they won't build us depth, but will let something appear, disappear, and reappear in a rug.

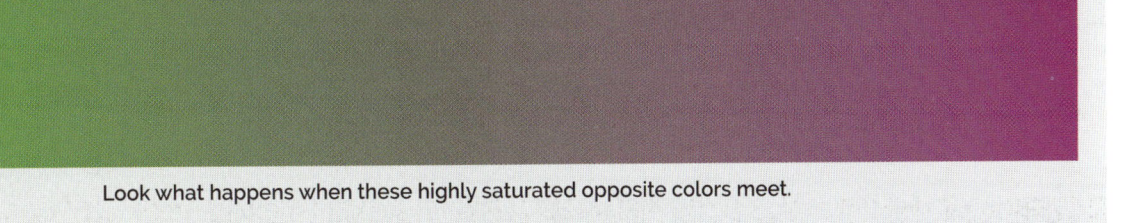

Look what happens when these highly saturated opposite colors meet.

Or this opposite set, not so saturated but still beautiful.

We can sometimes see the effects of the lack of values in transitions when we use dip dyes. Dip dyes don't always have dark enough values or light enough values to allow you to shade easily if there is more than one layer, or overlapping motifs in your hooking pattern. For example, when working with dip dyes, the medium values, which dominate a dip dye, will meet in the middle of each petal. If we are working petals or something that has layers and using dip dyes, it is best to make two dip-dye arrays: one with cooler, darker, and duller colors; and the other with warmer, lighter, and brighter colors. This way the cooler, darker, duller array can be used on the lower layer, helping it to recede. The other warmer, brighter, and lighter dip dye can be used on the top layer so it appears to move forward.

We can dye these beautiful color mixes shown in the diagrams. Imagine that the two colors we chose to use as formulas for this type of dyeing were dyes straight out of the jar. Now let's think about using opposite colors for dyeing.

Here I have used Blue as Formula One and Orange as Formula Two.

Saturation | 51

TOOL MAKING

Here's how you can play with these opposite colors, saturation cancelers, using the usual 6- or 8-jar dyeing method:

For Formula One, pick out one color of dye and mix 1/16 tsp. in two cups of boiling water. For Formula Two, find its opposite color and do the same.
1. Measure 1 Tbsp. of Formula One into every jar.
2. Next, measure out Formula Two into the same jars, using the following measures:

   Jar 1: 1 tsp.   Jar 3: 4 tsp.   Jar 5: 16 tsp.
   Jar 2: 2 tsp.   Jar 4: 8 tsp.   Jar 6: 32 tsp and so on...

1. Add 1/32 yd. of wool into each jar. Stir wool well.
2. Now, continue on with stirring (or not, as you choose) and processing as usual with swatch dyeing by adding acid at the halfway point of dye take-up. Stir occasionally until the water has cleared.
3. I had some fun with my example. I used 2 Tbsp. Formula One, (Blue) in each jar and used the following measures of Formula Two (Orange):

   Jar 1: 1 Tbsp.   Jar 3: 4 Tbsp.   Jar 5: 8 Tbsp.   Jar 7: 18 Tbsp.
   Jar 2: 2 Tbsp.   Jar 4: 6 Tbsp.   Jar 6: 12 Tbsp.   Jar 8: 24 Tbsp.

Keep in mind I did have to mix up quite a bit more dye because of my increased measurements. Note that I did not double the measures of Formula Two; making good values was not my goal.

THINGS TO HANKER AFTER

- Remember that bright and dull belong together as a concept to measure one aspect of color: saturation.

- Look for saturation leanings in your own work and stash, and try to lean the other way.

- Know that lessening the amount of color present in an object creates distance.

- Remember that saturation reinforces the message of value as we move away from objects, and that depth of field depends on saturation.

Don't be hard on yourself. This color concept is the least considered and least used in rug hooking. You don't have many good examples of saturation use to look at in hooked rugs, so start casting your eyes toward other art forms to see it in action.

Let's look at our color chip again:

Now we have color, value, and saturation identified.

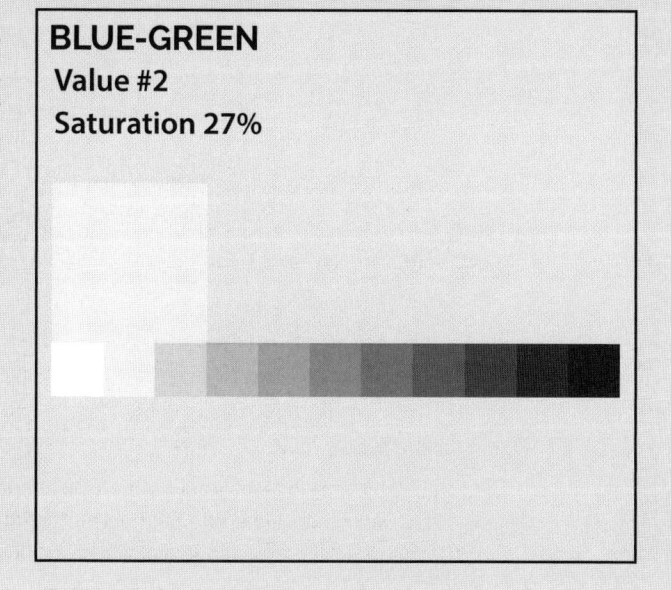

BLUE-GREEN
Value #2
Saturation 27%

52 | *The Color Lab*

JULIE'S FUN WITH SATURATION

WK: Julie, you have many different color saturations in *Value Study*. How did you find the right home for them?

JC: I have trouble figuring out where those brights go in a value piece like this rug. I use the black-and-white setting on my camera to see if the value is correct. Often the bright piece of wool looks like it would not fit, but I trust the black-and-white camera, and it is usually correct. I find that the very bright piece "fits in" better, depending on what goes in next to it. I don't seem to have this issue, to quite the same extent, with very dull pieces of wool.

WK: Do you know your favorite saturation points? Have you found them changing over the course of your hooking career?

Value Study, 27 1/2 " x 15", #4- to 8-cut wool on linen. Designed and hooked by Julie Cheeseman, Meaford, Ontario.

JC: I prefer medium saturation. I used to use a lot of very dull wool. Now I am more comfortable using wool with different saturations, and I like the look of that better. I am learning how to use brights so that they are effective but not overpowering. Of all the aspects of color, saturation is the one that I find the hardest to understand and to apply correctly.

WK: Can you tell us more about hooking this *Heron Rug*?

JC: I love watching the great blue herons in our yard in Florida. I have taken a lot of pictures of them over the years and wanted to try to hook one. I decided on the size for the rug and had the photo enlarged to that size, in black and white. The black-and-white image shows the different values more clearly than the color photo. Wanda convinced me to use only one picture as a visual. I wasn't too sure about that, but indeed it worked well. Under Wanda's guidance and with her dyed wool, I began hooking the bird according to the values I saw on my enlarged image and checking back with my color photo. I concentrated on value, temperature, and saturation. And I concentrated on shapes. This was tricky, because I always wanted to look at the bigger picture, but concentrating on shapes worked out in the end. This was a very challenging rug for me to hook. It was an incredible learning experience and I am very happy with the end result.

WK: Julie, I think it was your diligence that paid off in the end. We played a lot of saturation games in this rug. All of the sections of it—water, bird, rocks, grass, and leaves—have areas of bright and dull. This is what creates a realistic aspect. Well done!

Heron Rug, 25" x 38", #4- to 7-cut wool on linen. Designed and hooked by Julie Cheeseman, Meaford, Ontario. The "pattern" was from a photo that Julie took in her backyard in Florida.

Saturation | 53

5. TEMPERATURE

It's time to take our temperature, my friends, and look carefully at the last component of color. Knowing the temperature of any color can really boost your value and saturation choices. It is a tool that can imply light and darkness in new ways and help saturation speak deeply or shallowly.

Cool colors will recede and become back-droppish, while warm colors will advance.

Even at 10 percent saturation, only a few steps away from gray, with barely any color present at all, warm colors will stand out more than cool ones.

When I'm talking about temperature in this chapter, I'm leaving aside the old warm red/cool red, warm blue/cool blue, or violet, or green conversation for now. I'm only talking about the color wheel color temperatures. We will look at cooler or warmer parts of the same color family or how one hot color might look cool, in an upcoming chapter.

TWO IMPORTANT POINTS

First, I want to tell you two important things about warm and cool.

Every color on the color wheel belongs on the cool side of the tracks or the warm side. The cool colors on the right remind me of water: greens, blues, and violets. All the warm colors are on the left; I think of fire. They are red through orange to yellow, and those two wild cards of the color wheel, yellow-green and red-violet.

I've been asked how I know that. It is a good question. I can tell by the way they behave among other colors. Like all the warm colors, they advance to our eye. They rise up and move forward like things that are light and bright. They will never sit back like the cool colors.

I think of the color wheel as a party. We have red through to yellow attending this soiree. They are the hot colors, the party girls; they crave attention. They are not shrinking violets. They are the hot mamas of the gathering, and they make the party fun.

We have our purple to green color families coming too. They are shy. You might not see them at first because they are wallflowers. They are cold in their personality and even a little standoffish. They are subtle, deep-thinking, cool-customer types.

Of course, like real parties, there are always some celebratory hookups. Sometimes there are life-altering consequences. Yes, you've got it: offspring. These children are red-violet and yellow-green. You see, their momma was a hot color and their daddy was a cool one. They take after their momma, and her hot temperament rules out the cool. They, against their better judgment, are party girls too. Remember this: they will never act cool. As a matter of fact, they demand far more attention than the other warm colors.

The other important thing to remember is that orange is the warmest color and blue is the coolest color.

Colors Are

Warm   Or   Cool

54 | *The Color Lab*

Orange and blue are the poles of color temperature on the color wheel. Stepping away from either of them to the right or left moves us toward the opposite pole. When we are at orange, moving to the left or right moves us toward blue, drawing you toward cooler colors. Orange-red is moving toward blue and yellow-orange is also moving toward blue. If we are at blue, moving in either direction draws us closer to warmer colors. Blue-violet is moving toward orange and blue-green is also moving toward orange. Try this idea out by looking at our temperature color wheel.

Warmest and coolest colors: blue and orange

Temperature | 55

TEMPERATURE IN MY RUGS

So often the temperature in colors is ignored in rug hooking. We don't let this tool help bring things forward or recede. I use the concept of warm and cool a great deal as I make my rugs.

The colors in 85 percent of *Loon by Water* are cool temperatures. My skin is orange-based and warm, as are my scarf, my hair, and parts of the far shore. This cool surround brings an extra glow to my face. Along with being light, the warmth of color brings me alive.

56 | *The Color Lab*

In this journal rug, *The Circle of Life*, you can see the cool violet and green background is a great foil for the mostly warm or neutral motifs.

Peg Leg Footstool, #8-cut wool on linen. Hooked and designed by Wanda Kerr, Wiarton, Ontario. On this footstool cover, I'm playing warm motifs against a cool background. I called it *Peg Leg Footstool* because one of the legs is metal instead of wood.

Temperature | **57**

Here, in GOING DOWN THE TUBES, both warm and cool play an important part to create the sense of light. The darkest area is constructed of both warm and cool colors, a trick I often use.

DEARLY BELOVED, 31" x 26", various cuts and fabrics on linen, prodded and hooked. Designed and hooked by Wanda Kerr, Wiarton, Ontario. My heavy use of blue-green in this project called for a very warm sky to be a relief to cool temperatures.

This is my all-time favorite temperature-play rug. I balanced blue-green and green with red-violet and red-orange for lots of temperature bang!

All creations need temperature balance. A rug with all cool colors can be peaceful, but it could also be boring if there is no warm color present to add a spark or fire and to cool the cools even more. An opposite of any kind will vivify its partner. Red and green, light and dark, dull and bright, and warm and cool—all need each other to be the best they can be.

And the Day Came, 65" x 28", #8- and 12-cut wool, yarn, and nylons on linen. Designed and hooked by Wanda Kerr, Wiarton, Ontario.

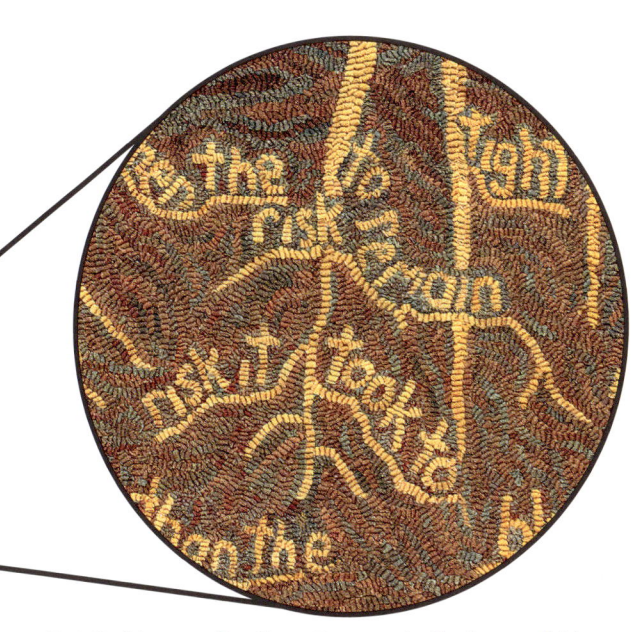

Detail of *And the Day Came*. Once again, the brown dirt is a warm and cool color combination. I've added depth to this color play by using my wandering method that creates layered colors by working with color temperatures.

Temperature | 59

Boat Lake Sunrise, #6- and 8-cut wool and nylon on linen. Designed and hooked by Wanda Kerr, Wiarton, Ontario.

Boat Lake is a winter scene with lots of grays, blues, and turquoises, but the wonderful sunrise and reflections warm up this dreary January day. You can see a glimpse of warm in the red-twigged dogwood shrubs along the shore. Can you see how the violet glimmer in the water looks a little warm? It is moving away from blue.

September is a temperature reversal to my footstool cover on page 57. The background is quite warm, and we see more cool in the wonky circles. This is the reversal of having a lot of cool colors. If you have a rug made up of all hot temperatures, it would be hard to look at. Blue, blue-green, and green, with a tiny smattering of violet appearing here and there, creates interest and balance.

60 | *The Color Lab*

This poppy pod is part of THE 3 STAGES OF WOMANHOOD. It has warm and cool colors. Look for the warm colors that form the ribs of the pod; they appear to stick out a bit. Cool colors make up the rest of the pod, the area under the crown, and under the pod on the stem. Playing with warm and cool created a bit of form. I didn't use much value change, so this warm/cool contouring is not noticeable from a distance. When will I ever learn?

HOW TO FIND A COLOR'S TEMPERATURE

When we discussed two of the other components of color, value and saturation, there was an area on those scales that was in between, sort of neutral, the medium value and the middle saturation point. In my experience, there is no middle ground with temperature. Colors are one temperature or the other. A color may look and act like a different temperature when it is being influenced by surrounding colors (read "It's All Relative", beginning on page 64, for more on that), but in isolation, they belong to one temperature or the other.

To determine any color's temperature, first decide which color family it belongs to, and then the temperature will be evident. As an alternative, think about the poles of blue and orange. Ask yourself: is this color moving closer to blue or moving closer to orange?

LAB WORK

DISCOVERY

Take a look at your stash. Do you have colors in it all the way around the color wheel? Most of us are missing one or two of the warm or cool colors. Which are you missing?

Find examples in your accumulated visual aids that show good balance of warm and cool.

Gather up a handful of strips. Look for the warm colors first—they advance to your eye. Pull these out. The cool colors will be left. You've just sorted colors into warm and cool piles.

Try hooking a sample of a color—yellow, for example. Hook yellow in the middle, and as you move to the left, add cooler yellows moving toward yellow-greens. On the right side, move toward warmer yellows such as yellow-orange.

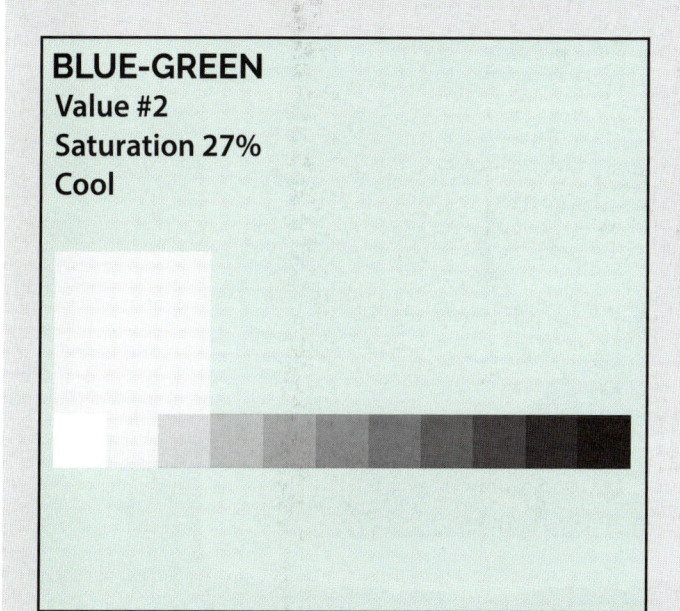

BLUE-GREEN
Value #2
Saturation 27%
Cool

Try introducing warm and cool into your personal color range. Think about color in terms of warm and cool, and strive for balance in your color planning. Look at works of art from other mediums to fine-tune your temperature balance. Study art to see how temperature is used to create balance and a sense of calm or impact.

Here I hooked samples of blue and red. In each circle, I moved to the warmer and cooler neighbors to complete my temperature exercise.

Temperature | 61

TOOL MAKING

DYEING WITH WARM AND COOL

Colors straight out of our dye jars can be a little bright for some. In an effort to turn down the volume on these colors, we have gotten into the habit of using a single dye to dull all colors.

Have you ever noticed how some colors lose their family hue when we do this? For instance, if we lower the saturation of blue by adding a brown, blue-green results. Thinking about temperature can prevent this family switch. To reduce the saturation of cool colors, add black. To reduce the saturation of warm colors, add brown. This keeps them living in the same house as the rest of their color family.

And thinking of temperature can enhance these family-switching effects. To get unusual colors from your dulling-down experiments, use warm colors to calm cool colors and cool colors to calm warm ones.

Even very light colors or very dark colors can be influenced by temperature. Blacks can be warmed, cooled, and brightened or dulled with 1 tbsp. of dye over 1/4 yd. of wool.

Look at your rugs to see if your color plans are crying out for temperature relief. Every color has a temperature and we can use this to our benefit. I often combine many temperatures in one background to highlight motif colors and give a sense of neutrality.

My wandering dye technique is a study in temperature-based dyeing. To find out about it and many other toothsome dyeing activities and hooking creativity, please go to The Welcome Mat at *www.thewelcomemat.ning.com*

The sample color we've been looking at is cool because it is blue-green.

THINGS TO HANKER AFTER

- Seek out ways to examine the concept of temperatures.

- Identify temperature in colors.

- Understand the pole principle: orange is the warmest color and blue is the coolest.

- Understand that red-violet and yellow-green are warm colors and are the most attention-demanding colors to look at and to use.

- Begin to play with temperature to embolden and balance your work.

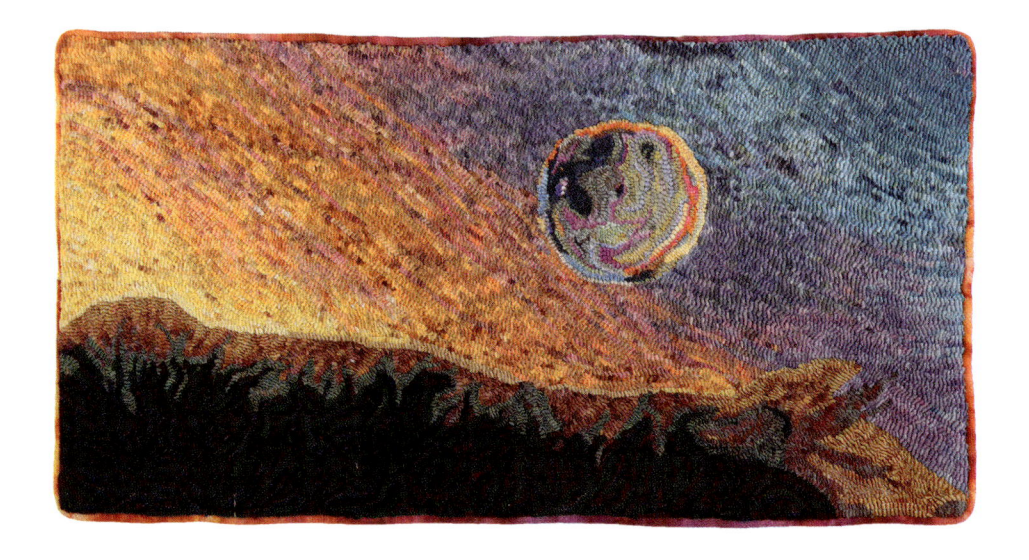

Julie and Temperature

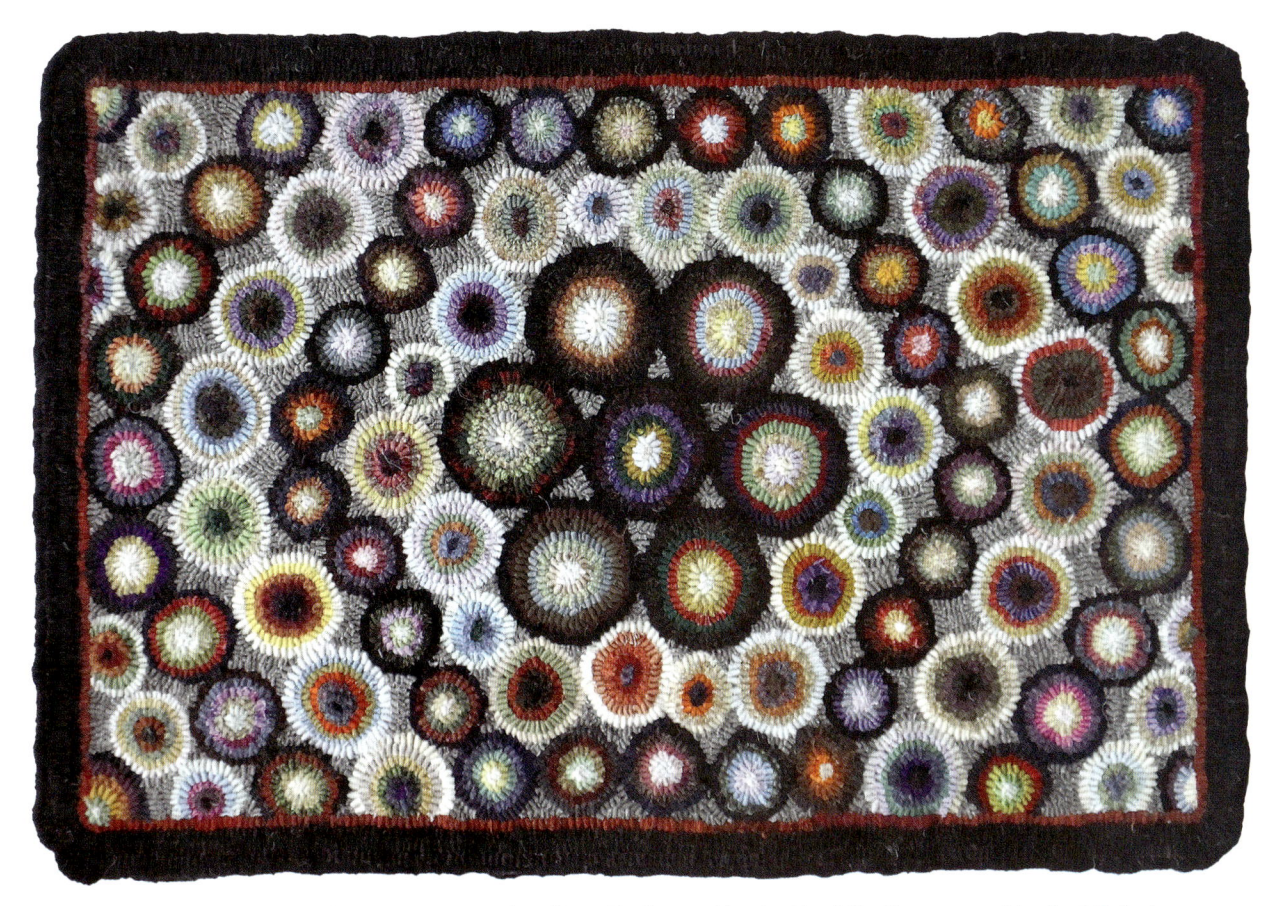

Small Change, 27" x 18", #3- to 8-cut wool on linen. Design and hooked by Julie Cheeseman, Meaford, Ontario.

JC: A "mini" challenge on The Welcome Mat was to create a few exercises with paper and pencil. I took a blank piece of paper and drew a few straight lines on the diagonal. I then traced some coins of different sizes—pennies, nickels, loonies, and toonies (Canadian $2 coin) over the lines. It made a really cool design. I wanted to explore "magnificent glow," as discussed on Our Weekly Bread on The Welcome Mat. I remembered my paper design from a few months earlier. I adapted the pattern, had it enlarged to the correct size, transferred it to linen, and started hooking. The pattern wasn't perfect in that the rug is not symmetrical. I thought this was going to drive me crazy because I LOVE everything to be symmetrical, but I pressed on and was happy with the end result. A hooking friend suggested the gray background, and it worked well. The same lady came up with *Small Change* for a name when I told the story, and I liked that too.

WK: Julie, you have great temperature balance in this rug as well as wonderful glow. I hadn't even noticed it was asymmetrical, as the color play is so much fun to look at.

Were you aware you were warming and cooling your circles as well, or was that a happy side effect of glowing?

JC: I wanted the outside of the circles to move from dark to light as they moved out. Inside each circle, I remember wanting to try "traveling"—moving from one color to another through the color wheel. I think this naturally changes the temperature. I was trying to start my circles with a different color/temperature and then fill. Sometimes that didn't happen, as I was watching for balance of the whole rug as well. I also paid attention to value and saturation; I think that helped create "glow" as I moved along.

WK: Julie, you are so right about the color wheel and glow. This is something we will study soon.

6. IT'S ALL RELATIVE: COLOR PLANNING

Now we are moving into a real game changer. In fact, everything I've told you is subject to change when we take relativity into consideration. That's why I might have called this chapter "Color: The Greatest Trickster of all Time."

Up to this point, we've been talking about what makes up a color—its four parts—and how they work together to create the hue we see. We've studied color or hue families, value, saturation, and temperature. As we did this, we were always looking at single colors in isolation.

Realistically, we don't work in this way with colors. While rug hooking, we rarely make anything with a single color; we often use 50 colors or more in a piece. It is almost as though we are casting a play when we create a rug. There are many colors uniting to create a single performance.

While we might look at a cast member as an individual, we won't know the impact they will actually have until we see them on the stage with the rest of the cast, acting their part in the play. In order to use color effectively, we must recognize that color continually deceives.

I like to say color is a language we all speak, but none of us understands what the other is saying. We have different perceptions about what colors are. To one person, a color is more blue-green; to another, more yellow-green; still another will see emerald green.

Why is this? The rods and cones in our eyes allow us to see color. Just like some of us have bodies that can run incredibly fast, have brains that are smarter than others, or are lovely and round-shaped, some of us can see color like a gorgeous, Olympic gold-medalist, Mensa member. Some of us are color-blind. Most are somewhere in between.

Nevertheless, I know we can all learn to use color effectively, with more efficiency and more powerfully (or should I say deliberately) than we do right now. The most seasoned color user and the beginner are equal in that we can all learn more.

Some people learn to play the piano with such soul and musicality that they can turn "Chopsticks" into a wonderful symphony. Then there is the player who can woodenly bang the song out. Both people are playing the same notes on the piano, and listeners can recognize what song is being played. But what a difference!

So it is with color, with each person using it to the depth and breadth of their own capabilities. We want everyone to recognize what they're seeing when they look at our work. We want them to hear our song no matter our level of virtuosity. Understanding color relativity helps our "color notes" ring true.

Relativity is a fascinating subject because color is so chameleon-like. I might choose a green that looks like the right temperature and seems perfect for my project. Once I surround it with a rich acid green, it turns toward blue. The same green, when surrounded by blue, might look more yellow-green.

Let's look at that green situation a little more carefully. We can make it appear yellower and almost disappear; we can make it look perfectly green; we can make it look dark or light; we can make it look blue and even bluer. All of this variation with the same color. Why is this happening? Every color is influenced by the colors it rests on, the colors that surround it, and the light that is depicted. A strong light in nature, and as depicted in art, removes color where it shines.

If I held up the blue-green color and placed blue behind it, the blue in the blue-green would disappear. What would happen if I held yellow behind it, or yellow-green? The first color, blue-green is completely influenced by the other color. It changes because it is relating to what surrounds it.

These are relative events with colors, shifts that happen when the actor is set on the stage among the other players.

Example of relativity, using blue-green as the center square in each block.

64 | *The Color Lab*

If I had one wish about color perception, I'd wish we could understand that no color stands alone. I might look at a color on my shelf and think, "Yes, you are dark." But then I see a pitch-dark black, and suddenly my chosen dark seems and looks like a lightweight; it might only be a #7 or #8 value. We could see this at work on my PRECIOUS sample below.

PRECIOUS, #12-cut wool, mostly wandered wool on linen. Designed and hooked by Wanda Kerr, Wiarton, Ontario.

A sampler of wool used in PRECIOUS, arranged by value.

Look at the top row, my value scale. I'm missing the darkest two values. I had not noticed the values did not go dark enough in that scale I dyed back in 2003.

Apparently, I was subconsciously aware of the need for the very darkest of values, (thankfully). You can see the proof of this. When I picked out the wool to use for PRECIOUS, I included black for both figures. The cat colors are below the value scale, and the girl colors are on the bottom row.

This happens on the light side of the value scale too. I find what I think is the perfect light color for a sky, only to hook it and have it appear dull and gloomy. I often see this result in hooked skies—the objects in the picture are lit up, but the sky is too dull for them.

Color always relates to what neighborhood it is in. Like a teenager, it might act completely differently at home or school, among friends, enemies, or relatives.

It's all Relative: Color Planning | **65**

Relativity events transpire with all parts of color. Light can become lighter when surround by a much darker color. The dark will look much darker when very light appears with it. Temperatures can be changed from warm to cooler, cool to warmer.

Look at the first block on the left. A warm color like yellow-green can look quite cool (even though we know it is a warm color), when surrounded by the warmest color.

In the second block, we see the same yellow-greens (one dull, one brighter), surrounded with cool colors. This yellow-green looks positively hot when it floats in a sea of cool blue-violet and turquoise (blue-green).

In the third block, we see the warmest color (orange) and the other warm colors as stripes. They look quite cool by comparison to orange.

See the block on the far right? The coolest color (blue) is surrounding other cool colors. These have transformed to look warmer in that blue cube.

Let's look at more color relativity at play with saturation. We can make a 50 percent saturated color look much brighter by surrounding it with areas of 0 percent to 30 percent saturation, or make it dull by surrounding it with very bright colors.

In this sample, we have a repeated color (violet) in the center of each rectangle.

- On the far left, it is surrounded with a very dark, warm brown; this makes it look lighter, cooler, and larger.

- Next, I surrounded it with a medium green, which makes it look warmer.

- When surrounded by blue, it looks grayer and warmer.

- Moving right, violet is surrounded by red-violet, making it look cool and duller.

- In a field of bright, light yellow, the violet takes on a cooler, brighter, and lighter aspect, and it looks smaller.

- In the midst of red–orange, the violet is cooler and grayer.

- Surrounded by the same value green, gray, and blue wandered wool, it disappears.

- In white, it becomes darker, smaller, and very violet.

This is color relativity in action: one color relating to other colors with many disguises. All the parts of color are subject to the effects of relativity. You can make almost any color act lighter, darker, brighter, duller, warmer, or cooler. You can even make a color act like it comes from another color family.

Planning out all the colors of your whole rug at once is important because relativity can throw an ad-hoc plan into ruination. Note the effect of using the opposite color in the yellow/violet example above. Yellow can appear incredibly electric by surrounding it with violet, too. An opposite color heightens any color's verve.

66 | *The Color Lab*

MY EXPERIENCE WITH RELATIVITY

Detail of *And the Day Came*

We can take any color and change the surroundings to create any effect we like with it. Artists have embraced this phenomenon since they started using pigment! As Eugene Delacroix once commented, "I can paint you the skin of Venus with mud, provided you let me surround it as I will."

I used this opposite color play in my rug *And the Day Came*. I wanted to see if I could have many colors appear red by the careful handling of green surrounding it. The poppies only have one true red in them. They have red-violet, red-orange, violet, orange, and even yellow and reddish brown making up their "red."

I made a multi-floral rug called *My English Garden* (page 68) and I wanted a #8-value eggplant background. I overdyed 1/4 yd. pieces of off-the-bolt eggplant with red, brown, orange, purple, blue, red-violet, turquoise, and yellow to allow some temperature change in this dark color. This way, I could play with the most suitable temperature to surround the multicolored flowers.

This rug has daffodils, which I chose to make yellow. I dyed to match a realistic daffodil yellow and did a pretty good job. When the swatch was laid against my background, it was electrified by its surrounding. We know yellow is a light color. Whenever we put dark against light we have vibrancy. Eggplant is part of the violet family, yellow's opposite color. This created another form of vibrant contrasting.

These glorious daffodils failed to fit in with my rug and its theme, even though the color was a realistic daffodil yellow. I had to overdye my swatch with black and kill that yellow to have the relationship between it and its background read true. While I was hooking it, a few people commented on the dead daffodil and why it was so dull, wondering politely if I thought it was the right color. The daffodil didn't have a color context without the stage hooked in, or as we refer to it, the background. Once the eggplant was hooked, the daffodil looked very reasonable, just like a daffodil should.

We are often encouraged to decide on the value of a background. Deciding if it will be light or dark helps us with value contrast on our motif edges. It is incredibly important to remember there is so much more to color than value.

This is why I think color decisions in rug hooking are best worked all at once. Knowing the background color exactly helps us make important temperature as well as saturation decisions in our motifs. It can help us reinforce value contrasts in artistic ways. We can use temperature and saturation contrast as well, and include opposite/complementary color play. This will help us cast the best play we can.

Relativity is one of the most important considerations as you choose colors for a rug.

Take your rug along when you shop or dye a new color for it. Reason flies out the window when we need to buy wool for one section of a rug, like water or the sky or background, or when we need to match something we ran out of. Unless we are endowed with the extremely special skill of a photographic memory for color, we will depend on our thoughts or feelings about what we need instead of what we really need. Take your project with you when you need wool. That's an important color rule!

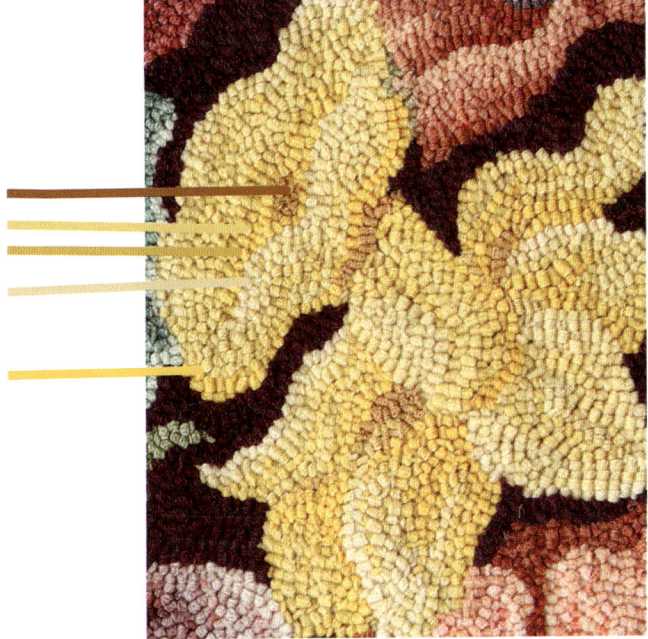

Detail of *My English Garden* and the true colors of the deadened daffodil. See full rug on page 68.

It's all Relative: Color Planning | **67**

My English Garden, 31" x 46", # 3-, 4-, and 5-cut wool on burlap.
Designed by Rittermere-Hurst-Field and hooked by Wanda Kerr, Wiarton, Ontario.

Joen Wolfrom's *Studio Color Wheel*   Courtesy of C&T Publishing.

Don Jusko's *Real Color Wheel*

WARM COLOR, COOL COLOR

Remember when we talked about temperature, and I said you'll have to wait to hear me talk about the warm/cool red situation? This is where the warm red and cool red, or any other color set, comes in.

In this "relative color" study, we are comparing a color to the rest of its family. Aunt Franny Red is expressive and warmer than reserved, cooler Aunt Catherine Red. They are both in the red family but are quite different in temperament. With this temperature relativity, we are looking for differences within hue families with little leanings toward orange (the warmest color) or blue (the coolest), which we can detect when the hue families get together.

We can easily see these leanings in temperature when we look at a color wheel made up of 24 or 36 colors, like *The Real Color Wheel* or *The Studio Color Wheel*. Hue relativity—how colors move from one hue to the next—is almost fluid. The more we divide the color wheel, the more indistinct individual hues become.

Let's look at some value relativity. Remember that every color has a value. The lightest colors are at either end of this sample and the darkest are in the middle. Hold this book at arm's length to gain some distance and take a look at what's going on.

- In the white row, the lightest color, yellow, doesn't really show up well, but the rest of the colors have good contrast.

- The middle value row has many disappearing sections. The gray obscures several colors, because they are of a medium value, and so is the gray.

- The black surrounding the colors on the bottom row diminishes the darker colors, all because of value.

Here is a sampling of the color wheel. The same colors are surrounded with black, white, and a middle-value gray.

It's all Relative: Color Planning | 69

Just to make sure you don't go haring off on a witch-hunt with pitchforks and axes after gray: this is all a matter of value. It's not a problem with gray as part of the color continuum. It is the relative effect of value. Most of the colors on the color wheel are in the medium value range. Each surrounding in our example—white, gray, or black—creates a particular change in the center color.

We don't always want to plan out our colors so carefully because a certain element of "surprise" or "scouting" for just the right fix (and I mean that in both ways) is mostly eliminated. Some of us live for that hunt. We might be instinctual hunter-gatherers, but thinking of the whole rug/relativity method has its rewards. It leaves more time to get hooking done rather than time spent hooking in and ripping out. Preplanning and making little value sketches, or color-scheme layouts showing the amounts of all the colors that will be used, can save you hours of time—time when you could have been dancing with your honey or hooking more.

RELATIVE COLOR IN VISUAL AIDS

When I'm teaching people to use photographic references and the work is filled with color, it can be overwhelming. I find it helpful for them, and for me, to have them seek out from the cast-off strip basket each color present in a visual they love.

This is the time when our prejudices appear. If we don't like light, we will see no light; it will not register with us even if it is present in our visual aid. The same goes for any other thing we dislike. (When you do this exercise with your leftover strips, you will also find out what you are missing in your stash.)

Often, we are so blind to our leanings we don't realize that the light or orange or very black area we overlook is the very thing that unites the beautiful visual we love. On the reverse side, I love to know exactly what a color looks like in a visual aid by itself. I like to weed out single colors, take them out of their context, to see what they really look like, away from the influence of relativity. I can be more accurate—doing this removes the guesswork and shows me baldly what the sought-out color is. It helps in dyeing too.

I do this with Adobe Photoshop Elements color picker. This tool replicates a color. It lets me seek and see any color in isolation.

For this project, I looked to see the values of one color present on the right. I see how it is in my hair and on the wall. I look for the quality of the lightest color present in the picture, on the right with a green cast and on the left with a blue cast. What is that color on my throat? How red is my lip shadow? This tool allows me to cut away relativity and my assumptions about what I see, bringing me closer to color accuracy. If we keep in mind the correct value, temperature, and saturation of a color, we can have more fun with hue.

Yes, my hair is brown and gray, but it also contains a cornucopia of delight: colors from shadows, highlights, and reflective colors. Even though I'm standing against a beautiful, creamy white wall and cabinet, you see no white in my photo. I must remain true to what I see, not what I know. I must choose grays and yellow-greens and red-violet to create my walls.

There is an old-school tool you can use too. To view color properly without a computer, create a color isolator. Cut a small 1/2" hole in thin cardboard to place over a visual, which allows us to see patches of the actual colors. This removes relativity and helps us pick more accurate colors. If we were hooking an orange, for instance, we may need to include brown, yellow-orange, yellow, or even white to create the round effect and shadows. The isolator lets us see this easily.

DYEING AND RELATIVITY

When I was hooking PEACE BY WATER, I ran from my dye kitchen to my washer and dryer to my hooking studio a hundred times, over and over, because I needed to brighten, or dull, or darken, or start again for a lighter version of a color. The colors needed to be just right. There are lots of areas where colors meet, and they run from lighter to brighter, they roll over to a neighboring color. So I needed an exact hue. I wasn't willing to settle for a "less-than" color. This was one rug where color interplay was incredibly important. I needed to have the water and sky lit up. I needed the sky to arc over me and the water to lie flat. Color did the work. I'm very glad I persevered to get just the right ones.

Have your rug close to hand while you are dyeing for it, and be prepared to re-dye! Wool in the hand is not like wool in the pot. It is lighter in the hand when dry.

PEACE BY WATER, 46" x 28", #12-cut wool on linen. Designed and hooked by Wanda Kerr, Wiarton, Ontario.

It's all Relative: Color Planning | 71

LAB WORK

Hook yourself a small sampler like I did for you here.

See if you can change a color's appearance by surrounding it with:

- A darker version of itself
- Something the same value, but not the same color
- Black
- White
- Its opposite
- A neighbor on the color wheel
- A brighter color
- A duller one

Look very hard at a visual you collected. Search for every color present. Match it to a strip of wool you have. Have you overlooked anything? Is your mind trying to master your eyes? Search hard to see what your ego wants to overlook. Take time to look closely; your destiny as a color master is there, just under the surface. Seeing colors in context and out of context will enable you to make more use of color, to enrich everything you do.

THINGS TO HANKER AFTER

- Understand that every color is a liar.
- Don't fall in love with any color until you see what kind of actor it is.
- Think about the "good, better, best" motto and endeavor to refine your choices.
- Actively seek out color revelation; look carefully to see what colors you need for any given project.
- Start to delve into more expressive color use.

THE THREE STAGES OF WOMANHOOD, 28" x 19", #12-cut wool, nylons, and chenille on linen. Designed and hooked by Wanda Kerr, Wiarton, Ontario. Here I played this game again in a background, this time with more subtlety, using duller colors and lighter values.

It's all Relative: Color Planning | 73

7. CREATING CONTRAST

Contrast is about differences. To create contrast is to create distinction between objects. In rug hooking, we often mislay the tool of contrast because of our love of hue and our innate desire to roll to the middle. Lack of planned contrasts results in work without a strong section that stands out from the others. Every rug deserves a leading lady. Contrast helps us create her.

When using color in design, we must bring some things ahead and let others recede. We need to create hard edges and soft edges. Contrast is just the enhancement our work needs. Everything in an artwork cannot be in sharp focus; it tires the eyes. And everything cannot be blurry—that is also tiring to view. In the first case, you long for sunglasses, and in the latter, you feel the need for reading glasses!

Contrast has three main expressions:

- Strong or high contrast creates a big visual statement. It makes hard edges. It shouts.

- Weak or low contrast creates blending situations and lets colors flow together like a whisper.

- Between these two polarities there is a middle sort of contrast. You can see differences. While they do not compel like high contrast, they do offer some distinction. They speak in well-modulated tones you can hear easily when in close proximity, but not if you are slightly removed.

Let's take a look at some contrast expressions in rugs.

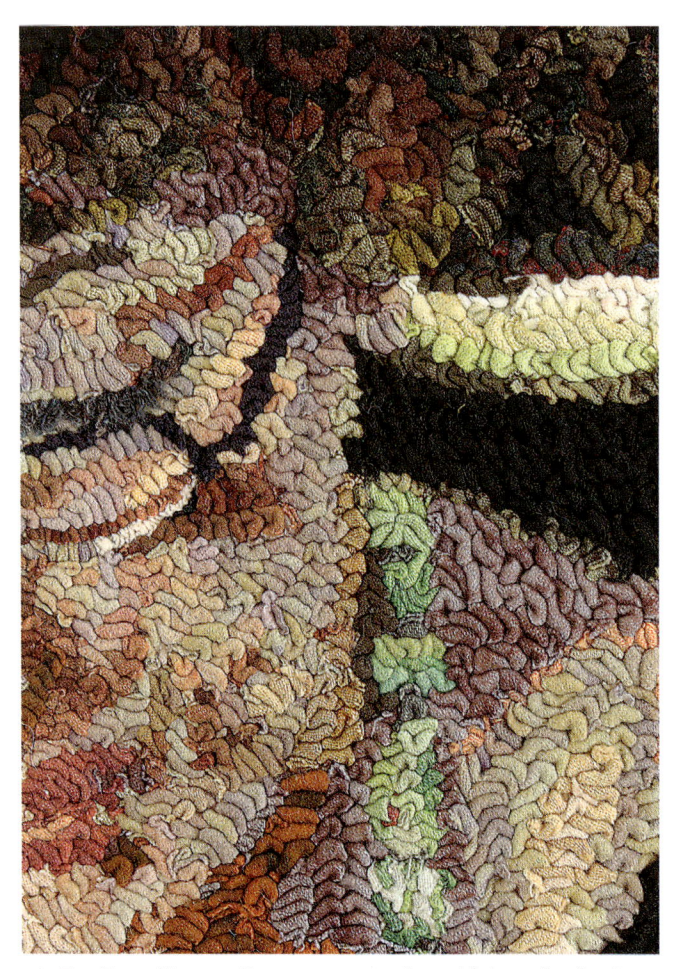

In *The Town Hooker*, there are areas of very high contrast using value: the black against white visible over my shoulder.

In *September Vogue*, warm against cool provides strong temperature contrast in the border containing the turquoise chain on the right.

The landmass in *Loon by Water* has very soft edges, low saturation, close values, and close temperatures.

74 | *The Color Lab*

There is a good balance of high and low contrast in this rug. It is singing a good song. Let's take a look for our middle-of-the-choir contrast, the one between high contrast and low contrast.

SEPTEMBER VOGUE, 31" x 49", #6-cut wool on linen. All motifs were inspired by the contents of the September 2009 edition of *Vogue* magazine. Designed and hooked by Wanda Kerr, Wiarton, Ontario. SEPTEMBER VOGUE also has some very soft contrasts in the middle field. Look for close values with similar saturations; only temperature in flashes of orange raises its voice a little. Soft contrast brings our eyes to a restful place in this rug.

IN A WORD, 28" x 59", # 8-cut wool on linen. Designed and hooked by Wanda Kerr, Wiarton, Ontario.

In this journal rug, very few things stand out loudly. I'm speaking my words a little quietly. If you look carefully, you'll see some words deliberately disappear. On the far right, look at the words in the first frond: Lay your plan. A quiet joke, for those who look closely, on the perils of not making a plan.

Creating Contrast | 75

HOW TO CONTRAST

How can we create contrasts on purpose—strong contrasts where we need them, soft where they belong, and middling to fill in between? When creating contrast with color, we have four main tools at our disposal. Yes, the same amazing tools we've been working with all through this book. These tools interweave, overlap, and are present in one way or another in every color.

To contrast we can use:

Contrast with Hue or Color Families: This category includes opposite colors for high contrast and colors close on the color wheel for low contrast.

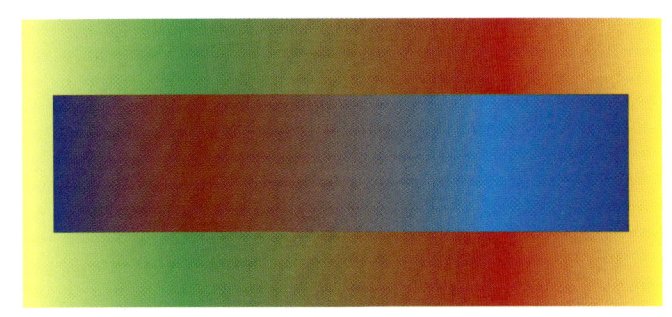

High contrast with hue  Low contrast with hue

Contrast with Value: Every color has a value, and value builds the framework of what we create. Strong value contrast builds healthy rugs.

Contrast with Temperature: Temperature can create contrast. Opposite colors create temperature contrast. Close temperatures create a low contrast. Neighboring colors provide a calming voice and simmer down the two opposites. This is an excellent trick to settle down loud areas in rugs.

High contrast with temperature  Low contrast with temperature

And the Day Came relies on temperature and saturation contrast. Looking at it in black and white, the key to value understanding, we see little contrast. Introducing higher contrast often involves two or more elements of color: hue, value, saturation, and temperature.

Creating Contrast | 77

CONTRAST WITH SATURATION:

This diagram shows us there is adequate contrast when bright meets dull. Value is a factor here too. Let's look at this diagram with the same value of colors at different saturations.

A darker dull gray surrounding the bright areas heightens the saturation of this strong color.

Here are the values in the second saturation sample. This contrast will not create strong bones.

What happens when we work all the components at once? In this color event, we have all of the varieties of contrast present: low, middling, and high. Hue, value, saturation, and temperature are all at work in this diagram.

78 | *The Color Lab*

Here is another way to look at contrast.

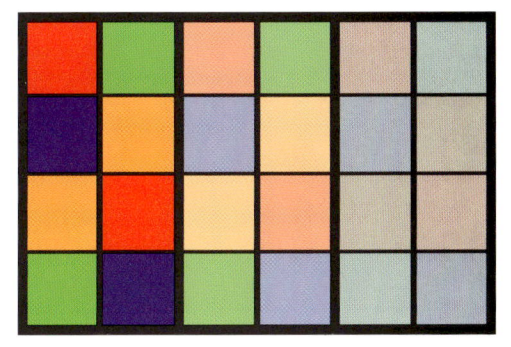

The first two columns have high contrast in hue, temperature, and saturation and some contrast in value. In the middle two columns, all of the contrast is reduced; mostly what we notice is temperature contrast. In the last two columns, we see all the parts of color blending in. Here we have low contrast.

High contrast is very important to include in any artwork, but if it is everywhere our nerves are jangled.

This contrast has both high and low parts. Does it seem a bit monotonous to look at? Do you know why? I think it is because of value.

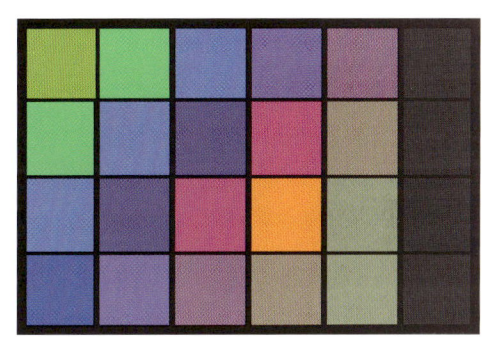

This contrast array is much more interesting. Changing some values from the middle to a bit lighter or darker created much more vivacity. Not too much light is involved here because, as you know, I'm a card-carrying Daughter of Darkness.

> *Color is a grand play-toy, my friends, and it keeps me endlessly amused. I've given you a cheat sheet for contrast.*
>
> » **TO INCREASE CONTRAST:**
>
> - Move colors four values away from each other.
> - Use opposite colors.
> - Increase temperature of one color radically, or decrease the temperature of another.
> - Increase saturation of one color, or drastically decrease the saturation of another.
>
> » **TO REDUCE CONTRAST:**
>
> - Bring stand-out colors closer in value to the others in their surroundings.
> - Decrease the saturations of colors.
> - Keep temperatures close; this naturally lets you keep hues close.

Creating Contrast | 79

Let's look at some hooked contrasts. I gathered a group of colors. First, I found sets of high-contrast colors and hooked them together.

High contrast is built from extremes: opposite colors, black and white, warm and cool, bright and dull.

Low contrast is created when I combine neighboring colors, which are naturally the same temperature, and I keep values and saturations close.

In this example, the high- and low-contrast partners switch dates, so the contrasts are more defined than low contrast, but not as loud as high contrast. Isn't it amazing how different they look once they are rearranged?

80 | *The Color Lab*

THE TOO-BUSY SYNDROME

Often, you'll hear a rug hooker remark that some pattern or another is too busy; it has too many lines and too much "stuff" on it. I guess they are imagining that everything in a complex rug will be hooked in high contrast. Contrast is reporting for duty to solve this problem for you.

We now know that we can use contrast to bring some areas into strong relief and have others fade into the background. "Busyness" is not in the lines of rug patterns; it is in the way we choose to color the pattern. "Busyness" is a cuss word to me.

Let's take a look at the old checkerboard pattern, well known for its distracting element of opposing squares. Do you see my point that there is no such thing as busy? There is only the lack of color imagination and not understanding the concepts of contrast.

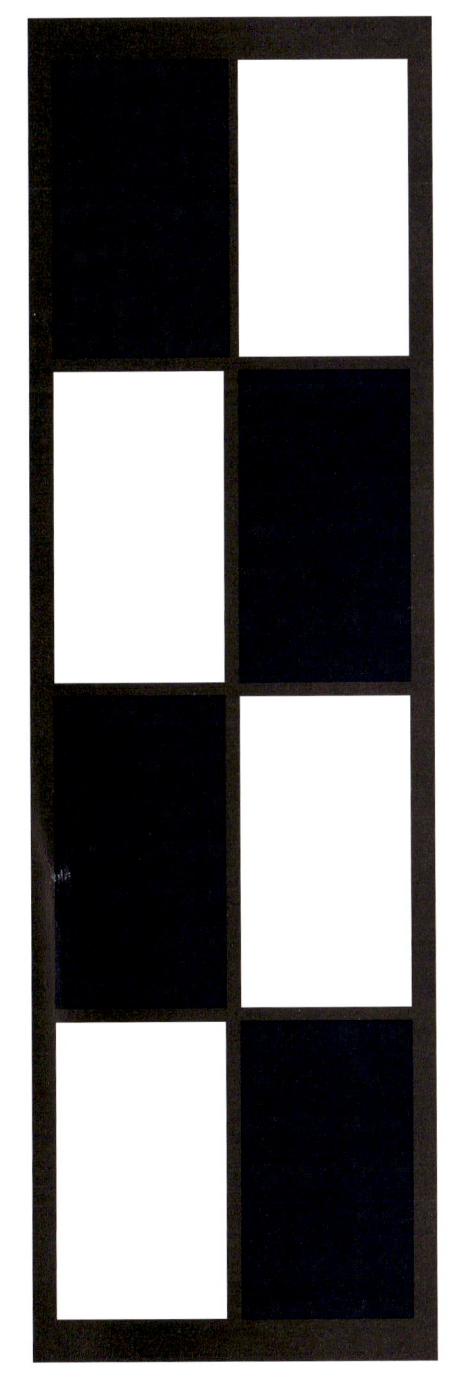

In black and white, it has contrast worthy of a national flag.

These neighborhood colors soften the pattern considerably.

Look at this low contrast checkerboard, my friends. It's as soft as a kitten!

Creating Contrast | 81

LAB WORK

BLENDING—WORKING IN LOW CONTRAST

This is a trick for using up scraps and developing areas of color that contain many colors but read as one. This trick will allow us to create magic from what we have on hand. Our scrap basket is an unsung hero.

I want you to create circles—or whatever shape you like.

- Go to your pile of cut strips. Grab a good quart-sized bag and fill it randomly.

- Sit down at a table and begin to sort them as you would laundry.

- Pull out the lights and place them in one pile.

- Pull out the darks you see and make a pile of those.

- There will be a medium value pile of wool remaining.

- Look at your light pile. There will probably be a range of lights: very light, medium light, and slightly darker lights. Make piles of each of those. At the very least, you will have two piles of light values.

- Now, examine that bunch of lights to find which one contains the most hues. (You can go back to your scraps to look for other colors of matching light value that you can add to bulk up the color variety.) This light circle needs to have all colors in it to be pearl-like.

- Hook a light-valued circle containing many hues.

- Next, hook a circle of medium, and then a circle of dark, going through the same sorting for one value with many colors as you did with the lights. The greater variety of same-value colors you hook into your circle, the richer the results will be.

Your circle might look something like this. This sample is many years old, and I see some colors in the middle value have faded to be a little lighter. Take a step back from your value circles. You know you have succeeded when the colors disappear, and the overall value prevails. Squinting works, too.

You might find you are a Daughter of Darkness and have few lights. I'll be frank; that time of frivolity has to come to an end if you want to make amazing work and fulfill your destiny as an artist. Meanwhile, until you can mend your wicked ways, borrow some strips from a Sister of the Light. Once you master this trick, your rug hooking can become luminous with beautiful opalescence. This will draw your audience in like jazz draws tourists to New Orleans.

LAB WORK

WORKING WITH HIGH CONTRASTS

It is fun to try hooking some high-contrast color samplers too. Try using our circle again, and hook rings of fighting colors. Use bright against dull, light against dark, warm against cool, and opposing hues as well. Knock 'em out!

High-contrast samples usually end up looking uglier than sin. Grin and bear it. You'll benefit from the ability to make something that shouts. Exercising your bold contrast muscle helps you be showier in areas you want to advance to the eye.

LEARN TO IMPLEMENT THE FADE

Contrast is the tool we use to let something appear and then fade out. When I was creating COLOR CONTRADISTINCTIONS, a journal rug, I knew I wanted to concentrate on strong contrast. In a journal rug, I look at daily representations of my ideas. As I reached the 26th day I saw my rug needed a pathway of calm. I saw that my sets of color twins were mostly saturated and my eyes and rug called out for some disappearing motifs.

Look at the middle of COLOR CONTRADISTINCTIONS (page 84). You will see a section where it appears there are no blocks. But look carefully: there are 5 blocks that are barely visible. They fade into the background.

In another journal rug, SEPTEMBER VOGUE, I also needed a calm area, so I let a week of motifs become part of the center field, all in very low contrast to the background.

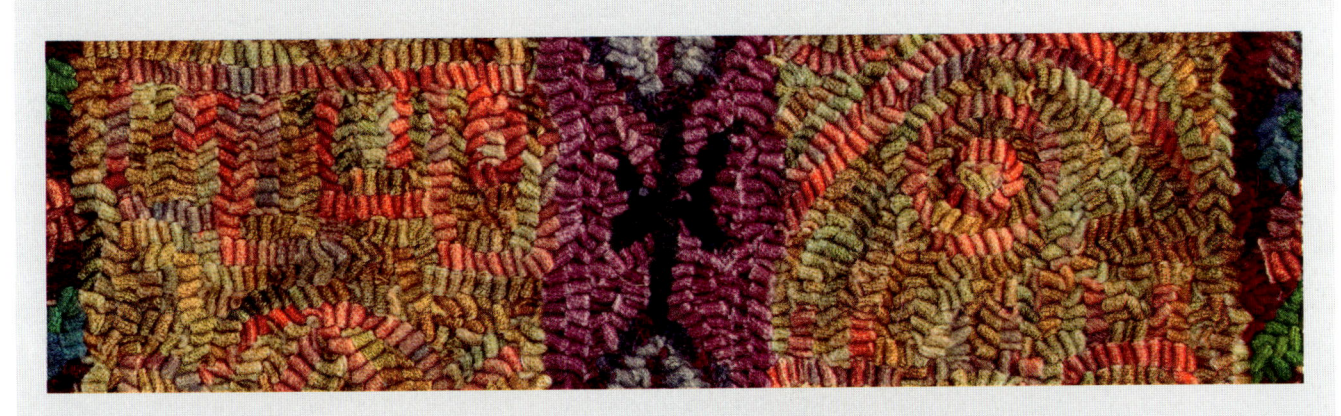

The fade can entertain and tickle your viewers. Letting edges of leaves or other objects fade into the background is a clever trick to help one's focus be drawn to more important motifs. It is great to practice using the fade so we learn to do it deliberately instead of as the result of haphazard choices.

We can often see this fade effect in fabric samples. There is so much to be learn from looking at everyday printed items like our sheets or shirts. There are often three artwork layers with fabric. They consist of a layer we focus on, the one on top. Then there is a second layer which supports the object on top. Then there is the layer that builds between the support layer and background. This "fade layer" helps draw us back into the background. Objects in the fade are muted, close to the background, not showy at all.

To practice the fade, draw three flowers that overlap. Let the top one be most powerful in color. Let the second layer move away from the viewer—it supports the show girl. Then make a fading flower with the third layer, the one on the bottom, the one you drew first. Keep it fairly close to the background in color, value, temperature, and saturation—but be sure to let the flower have some presence. It is a bridge between the support layer and the background.

This technique also helps us develop and understanding of depth of field when rendering landscapes.

Creating Contrast

LAB WORK

Color Contradistinction, January Journal, 48" x 36", #8-cut wool on linen. Designed and hooked by Wanda Kerr, Wiarton, Ontario.

LAB WORK

CONTRAST AND WEIGHT EXPERIMENTS

I encourage you to occasionally create a study rug or sample journal. I have learned much more from doing journal rugs than I ever have making any other kind of rug. These pieces are the places where I can follow my whims and instincts with not a care in the world. I just let color play out as I'm inspired to.

In January 2017, I made a rug where I studied the effects of the amount of two contrasting colors have when used in a shape. In the first shape, a rectangle, I used color #1. Into that first field of color, I put a stamp shape of color #2. Then I reverse the rectangle and stamp's colors. I was curious if relativity (aka simultaneous contrast) would create the same effects in both samples. I was excited to see that size did matter and affected the color's interactions.

COLOR CONTRADISTICTION, seen on the facing page, is the result. It is fun to hunt for the partners where the colors are reversed.

THINGS TO HANKER AFTER

- Take contrast into consideration.

- Understand that "busyness" is a concept you can control with contrast.

- Grasp the four ways to use contrast for low or high effects.

- Use the cheat sheet to help you with your rug problems.

Detail of ONE DAY ONE LINE. Working with many levels of contrast is deeply satisfying to me.

Creating Contrast | **85**

8. CREATING TRANSITIONS

Color transition is when one color moves in a logical way to another color. What does this look like? From one hue to another, a rainbow is a hue transition. See the logical movement when we travel from blue-green to green-yellow to orange-red in this example? The colors move around the color wheel.

Yes, a rainbow is a color transition. These color flows can also be called gradients.

All four parts of color can be transitioned.

Here is a quiet-hued gradient, so different from the bright rainbow above. This is a quiet color transition.

We can travel along values from light to dark.

We can move along the saturation scale from bright to dull.

We can travel from one temperature to another.

Transitions are beautiful, and the natural world is full of them. Gradients are everywhere we look. We see the back of a rose petal with colors running from burgundy to pink, a leaf changing from green to yellow to orange, then to red in the autumn. The plumage of a bird, the elegant shift from shallow water to deep water, the miracle of a sunrise or sunset, and the spectacular oil-slick carapace of a beetle—all of these are beautiful color transitions.

86 | *The Color Lab*

GOOD TRANSITIONS

In beautiful transitions, colors will travel smoothly. Sometimes I call working with this kind of color play traveling, because we are traveling from one spot on the color continuum to another.

Be aware of opportunities to apply transitions. This lets us create wonderful connections between our colors. The ways we choose to do this are varied; we can really present a unique color style in our rugs if we are brave enough to chase the idea of color transitioning.

How this might work in your rug? Let me explain.

- Instead of making a tree trunk plain gray, you might travel from gray blue on one side of the tree to a darker gray brown on the other.

- Or you might see a repeated pattern of a geometric and decide to move the background behind it from one color to another, while filling in the main shapes with a silhouette's single color.

- Imagine for a minute that the repeated motifs in your Oriental border had color play along them. We would see the rug edge motifs filled in with colors moving from blue green through blue to blue violet and back again. We could transition colors running top-to-bottom or side-to-side in each motif.

- Can you imagine a hooked morning sky stretching through yellow to peach to pink to violet, and then to blue?

I use gradients constantly in my color work. Creating smooth transitions is one of the best tricks I know. Imagine you are hooking a portrait and need a blue-violet iris in the left eye and a green iris in the right eye because of lighting. What colors might you use in both eyes to unite them?

This is the joy of how to transition: asking questions. The questions to ask are simple.

- Where on the color wheel do I want to start and end my transition?

- What are the possible routes between these two colors?

- Which direction around the wheel should I take?

You can travel from any color to any other color in either direction, but the results are quite different. Make sure you know the core color you want to emphasize. Going one direction around the color wheel will work better than the other for your purposes. Examine both to be sure.

In this diagram, we move from violet to green via the shortest route around the color wheel. This transition will be mostly "blue" looking and coolly colored.

Traveling between the same two colors in the opposite direction around the color wheel, taking the scenic route, creates a remarkably different transition. This one appears mostly warm, it has a strong glow from moving through the lighter colors, and it is almost prismatic.

Creating Transitions

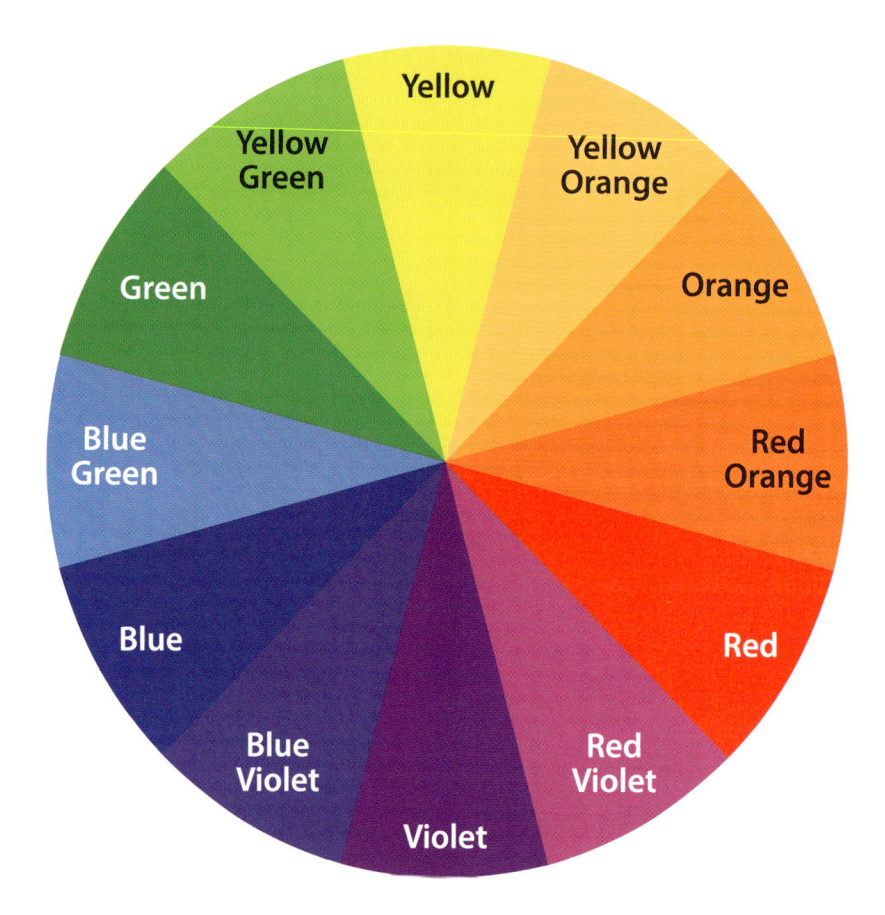

Let's try out a gradient idea with the iris problem we mentioned before. Look at blue-violet, and then look at green; which colors lay between? This is where you will search for your transition answer—in those color families between. The answer is blue and blue-green; they sit between the blue-violet and green you are looking to transition.

You will need to look at the values and saturation of the blue-violet and the green, and work to keep them somewhat congruent, in order to have a smooth and beautiful flow.

Blue-violet travels to green through blue and blue-green. Adding the two in-between colors unites the hooked eyes and they belong to each other. It provides the delightful surprise of color mastery for those who look closely. More is more.

Most artists who work with many colors, like pastel artists, or colored pencil artists, keep color families together so they have readily available sorted selections of color to draw from. We should follow their lead.

Oy! Our leftover cut strips, those strips we have discarded and shunned, will prove so useful to you in your color discoveries—search through them and find just what you need! Remember back in our hue chapter I suggested that you sort all your cut strips into hue families? I was recommending that you organize your stash, and there are some great reasons for this suggestion. Sorting will develop your color chops and supply you with ready-made fodder to try out these new color ideas!

88 | The Color Lab

COLOR TRANSITIONS IN RUGS

Transitions can happen through the four aspects of color we have been discussing: hue, value, temperature, and saturation. We have already seen transitions present in the color wheel, the value scale, the saturation scale, and through looking at temperature. Usually, several of these are operating at the same time.

We use transitions when we work with a swatch. This tool, a swatch, is a value transition. We can organize any collection of wools in a similar swatch arrangement to use in the transition of color and value.

Let me say that again: We can shade anything without a specially dyed swatch. Using an "assembled swatch," as this technique is dubbed by the glorious Maggie McCrea, is a fantastic way to bring some spark to shading.

In my online class, Painterly Poppies, we used this assembled swatch idea to hook the class pattern. Here, I gathered a simple color transition around the red neighborhood: a variety of violet to orange-red wools. You can see that they all fit in with one another, even though some are brighter or duller and some are lighter or darker. It is a lively way to shade. You can do this with any three-dimensional object you wish to have form.

I settled on these "reds" from the wider array for my first flower.

See the assembled colors doing the work of creating form?

Here is another flower in the same rug using slightly different colors to complete its value transition, moving from darker red-violet, to red, to red-orange, to orange.

Use any method of shading: fingering, feathering, fans (as in ruffled petals), and elles (end, loop, loop, end.) Even if you aren't interested in shading, you can find simple pleasure and great reward in moving from one color to another in your project. As humans, we love gradients, and we look for them.

Creating Transitions | 89

Transitions make our hooking work more artistic. Let's look at some more transitions.

We are transitioning from warm to cool, bright to duller, and staying pretty much in the same value.

Here we travel from medium to light to medium values, through the warm colors, yellow-green to orange-yellow. Notice how this sample travels from a cooler warm to a color closer to our warmest color, orange. We also have a bright highlight in the middle.

In this transition, we travel from light to dark, through the color wheel, warm to cool, and back to warm again. We also shift in saturation from 80 percent at the yellow end to about 55 percent at the yellow-green end. What a beautiful trip!

Here are some of the transitions I've created in rugs.

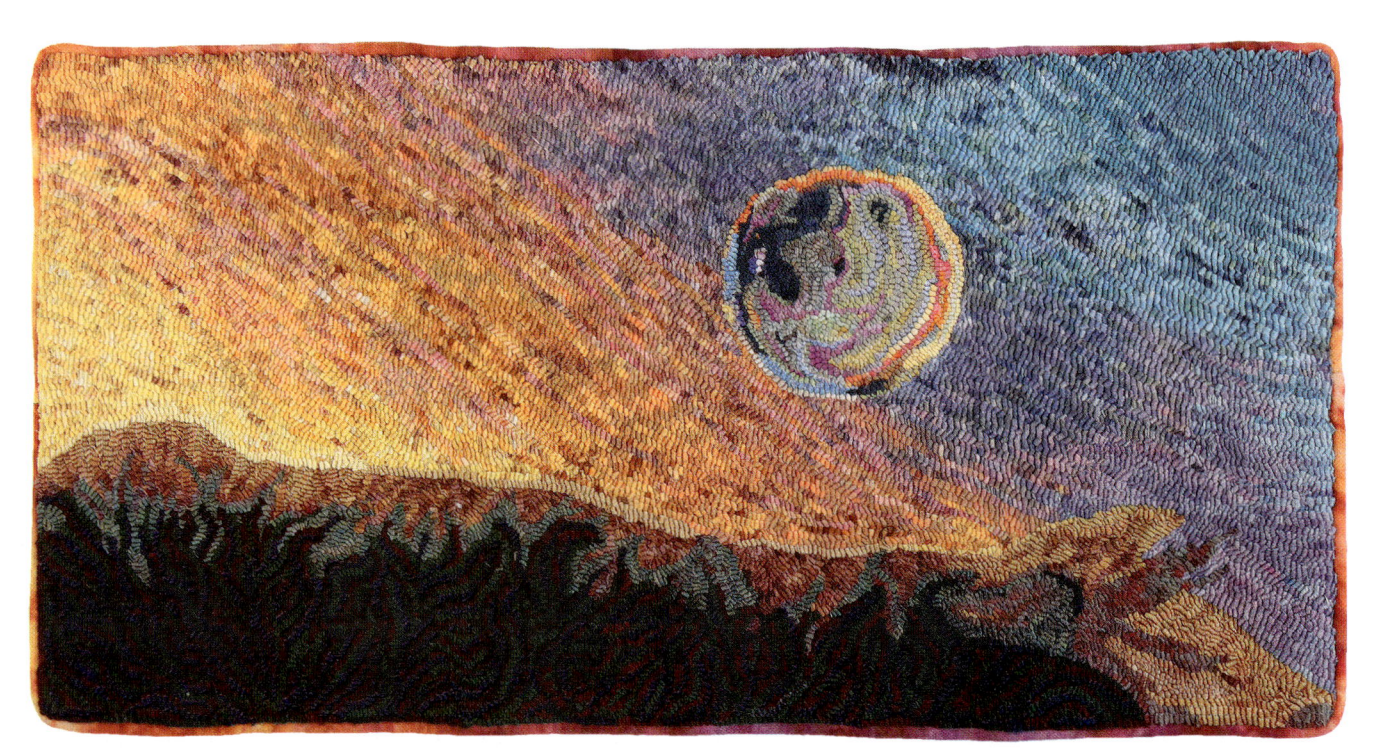

In *Going Down the Tubes*, I built a colorful speckled background that runs from yellow through orange to red-violet to violet, into blue, and then blue-green.

90 | *The Color Lab*

Circle of Life, 34" x 26", #8-cut wool on linen.
Designed and hooked by Wanda Kerr, Wiarton, Ontario. Value plays an important role when you transition with colors. It backs up the hue movement when you keep values and saturations similar. A dull color can do a lot to help you change to a new color. You can see blue and blue-green pop up very briefly as I moved from green to violet. This rug has many flowing transitions in its background. The colors move from lighter to darker, green to violet.

In this landscape, the water moves from lighter green, to blue-green, to blue, to blue-violet, and then to violet at the far shore. It grows duller as it moves away.

Creating Transitions | 91

THE SPIRIT MOOSE, 18" x 15", #12-cut wool, yarn, and nylons on linen. Designed and hooked by Wanda Kerr, Wiarton, Ontario. This rug was made entirely from leftovers remaining from my *IF BY WATER* series of rugs. In it, you can see me working these scant available colors to make up the moose's body. These are not as smooth as I might desire, but there is a certain spirit about the color use.

MIC MAC, 43" x 24", #3- and 6-cut wool on burlap. Designed by House of Price and hooked by Wanda Kerr, Wiarton, Ontario. I have several gradients working in *MIC MAC*. Scrolls change color with their inner line, the background is a value gradient, and the fish change color slightly each time they appear. All of these transitions create eye candy.

92 | *The Color Lab*

ONE ROW ONE DAY, 45" x 15", #4-, 5-, and 6-cut wool on linen. Designed and hooked by Wanda Kerr, Wiarton, Ontario.

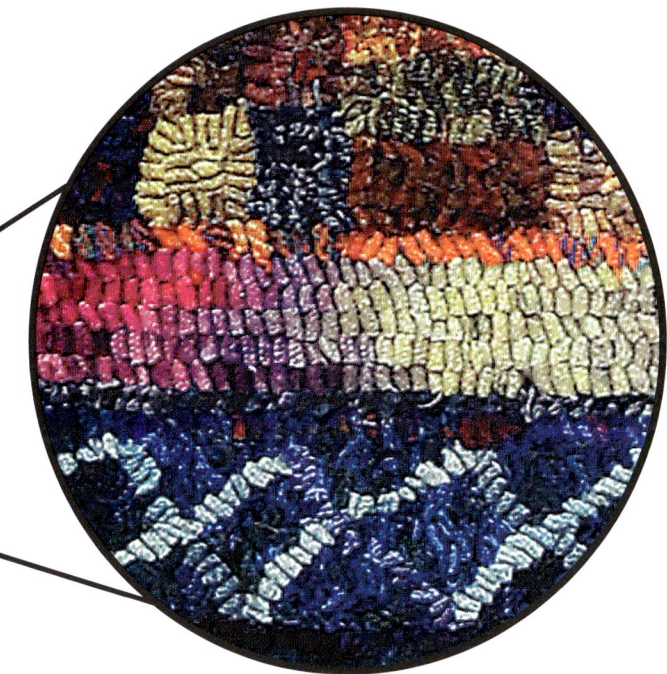

In this journal rug, gradients aren't grandly displayed; they appear in smaller ways and make the rows more interesting to look at and to hook. Look for some transitions: Can you see things change to other colors along a row, or lose saturation? Maybe you see colors getting lighter or darker, or warmer or cooler. Take a good look. Gradients can be large, like those in backgrounds, but they can also be small glimmers in your work. Even the tiniest of transitions make magic.

Creating Transitions | 93

I dyed the wool for this small piece, CELL BLOCK #9. One ¼ yard piece of transitionally dyed wool in a method I call "Go Your Own Way," with four or five different colors, makes up this background. The cell walls are also a long transitionally dyed piece of wool, what I call a "long and lovely." Careful handling of both wools was needed so that like colors pooled together.

In this detail of INTERSECTIONS, we see many small transitions between two colors.

Can you picture a winter's dawn in this transition?

You can make terrific traveling gradients in an electric skillet. Use the same approach you use to travel between any two colors, but do it with dye. The skillet allows quick handling of the dye process. You can add one dye at a time and let it almost take up, and then add another dye and then another in this same way, blending the colors one by one. This reduces the chance of turning rich colorations to mud.

Sunrise/sunset transition. These are two transitions that meet. On the top is a morning sky. The sun rises and the colors shift to yellow . With the day's passing, sunset comes with all of its beautiful transitions. We end with the evening sky. Both of these transitions were dyed using my One Pot Parlay method.

Creating Transitions | 95

LAB WORK

Do you remember the ways you can create transitions using color?

- You can travel around the color wheel by hue.

- You can travel from light to dark, or dark to light.

- You can travel from dull to bright, or bright to dull.

- You can travel from warm to cool, or cool to warm.

More than one of these "travelings" can happen at the same time.

Let's look at some more gradients. Can you identify what is transitioning in each grouping? Remember that sometimes there are two or more components moving at once.

These are the questions you need to ask yourself when creating a gradient:

- Where on the color wheel do I want to start and end?

- What are the possible routes between these two colors?

- Which direction around the wheel should I take?

- Which parts of color, hue, value, saturation, or temperature do I need to use to make a smooth transition that creates the effect I want?

I want to be honest with you: a person can read about this until the cows come home. (If you aren't aware of this, cows will not come home by themselves!) Reading and looking will not help you know or understand this. You must do it.

Search through your sorted strips for an area of the wheel where you have plenty of selection. Try making some tiny transitions. Just travel for short four rows.

96 | *The Color Lab*

LAB WORK

Next try drawing something you are used to hooking. I chose a leaf. A painterly leaf. Notice how I transitioned in this leaf. Traveling from bottom to top, I went from dark to light. Moving side to side, I traveled from warm to cool. These colors were all drawn out of a scrap bag of leftover green wool strips. I call this kind of hooking "painterly" because of the qualities imparted by using value with a multitude of dull, bright, warm, and cool greens.

THINGS TO HANKER AFTER

- Know that color is a tool you can manipulate.

- Create some gradients.

- Begin to see the value in creating with color in new ways.

- Be more painterly and inventive with your color use.

- Add transitioning to your hooking tool box.

Creating Transitions

9. CREATING GLOW

In the last chapter, did you notice how some of the transitions appear to be lit up by light? Transitioning brings us directly to the glorious color trick of glow. Making something glow is one of my favorite color tricks. I think our work needs this special element. All creatures are attracted to glow and sparkle.

Do you know what I mean by glow? It is a word I use to describe a slow lightening, warming, or brightening of an area. Glow happens in those sections of an artistic work that appear to be a source of light, like the sun as it sets or stars at night. A candle flame glows, and a bonfire glows. We can have glowing areas in floral subjects and geometrics. We can even have glow in primitives. We should always have glowing areas present in portraits to bring our subjects to life.

There are four ways to create glow using our color tools. Most often, we will use two or three of the tools together to create glow.

- We can move from light to dark using value.

- We can move from bright to dull.

- We can move from cool to warm.

- We can move around the color wheel in transitions, providing these transitions include something light and dark, such as moving from yellow (a naturally light and warm color) to blue (a naturally darker, cooler color).

Value glow

Saturation glow

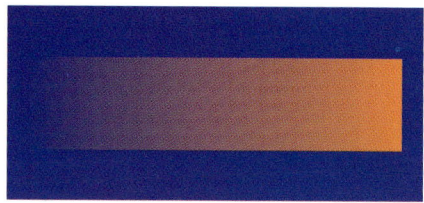

Temperature glow

Hue glow with white background

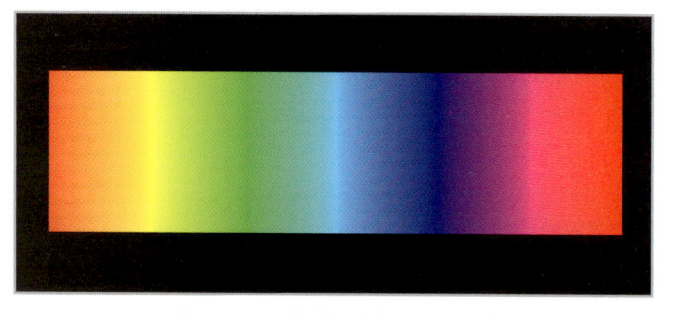

Push yourself to achieve glow. If you aren't for exaggerated values, you may feel quite bilious at forcing it. But the results in your work will be wonderful.

Remember that one area should be "glowier" than all the rest. You might have some reflected glow from this area, but you need one place where you locate your prime glow—one section in your work needs to shine above all others. If I were talking of a daytime landscape, I might tell you to look at your sky as the source of light and glow. This sky should illuminate above all others, and be the prime source of light. Skies often are lighter and brighter than we might imagine. Even on gloomy days, the sky glows lighter and brighter than anything else. It is the prime source of light.

Glow requires dark to be present. Look at the example on the left of hue glow. Do you notice that there is more luminosity with the black surrounding it than with the white? Think of the sun or the moon in the midday sky. We can't quite perceive of the moon's wonderful light during the day; the values of the moon and sun are too close in value to the daytime sky. But as night approaches, during sunset and night, they positively glow.

Hue glow with black background

98 | *The Color Lab*

HOW I WORK WITH GLOW

Here are some examples of glow spots in my rugs.

Magnolia Chair Pad, 16" x 16", #6-cut on rug warp. Pattern by Jane McGown Flynn for Charco, hooked by Wanda Kerr, Wiarton, Ontario.

The red-violet line is the same value as the background but is a temperature change. This allows the line to glow. There is a great build up from dark to light. Moving from dark to light is a direct and easy path to create glow.

The way I've hooked a dark border and a slightly lighter background, a still lighter leaf set, and then a quite light flower created glow. Also, we can see some saturation glow. The dull leaves against the brightness of the red-violet petals (party girl!) make great glow. The colored line between the border and background did not compete strongly with my glowing flower because of the value I chose. Looking at it in black and white, we can see the value information.

A Story of Glow

We are all blind to our own work while it is being made. That's the bald truth of creation. And sadly, sometimes we do not wake from the dream of beautiful rendering to see what is before us in the light of day. Luckily, in this case, I did.

Spirit Owl, 18" x 12", #6 and 8-cuts on linen. Designed and hooked by Wanda Kerr, Wiarton, Ontario.

Spirit Owl with corrected sky glow.

I'd like you to meet my *Spirit Owl*. I have a series of Spirit Animal patterns on The Welcome Mat for members to hook if they wish. See that beautiful area in the upper right? That's my glow. But, mysteriously, it does not stretch across the sky. What? So weird! I pulled out some sky on the left and made it part of the glow. The photo on the right shows the glow corrected with my paint program. I hooked the glow as I have it painted and I felt much better about my work.

Repose, 20" x 14", nylon stockings on linen. Designed and hooked by Wanda Kerr, Wiarton, Ontario.

My daughter sits in front of her laptop and uses Photo-Booth to capture her image late at night. The light shines straight from the screen. The camera cannot catch depth, and so it focuses on the area closest to itself. Therefore, the edges of her hands and her nose are in sharp relief. We see the brightest glow in those spots, too. This glow would not prevail if I had used a light background; it is dependent on darkness. She was wearing black, so all of her clothes are "lost" in the darkness.

LONE PINE, #3- to 6-cut wool on linen. Designed and hooked by Wanda Kerr, Wiarton, Ontario.
Available as a free class and pattern on The Welcome Mat

The sky in *Lone Pine* is hooked with wool dyed by using the wandering method. Hooking with wandering wool will naturally provide quiet sparkle with its soft areas of lighter and brighter colorations. I invented this dye method to help us create more painterly ways of using color while hooking. If we wish to, we can apply subtle sparkle all over an area of a rug in this way. I have a name for this quiet glow: I call it "glimmer."

Creating Glow | 101

NINE OF SPADES, 20" x 28", #8-cut wool, yarn, and nylon, on linen. Designed and hooked by Wanda Kerr, Wiarton, Ontario.

The glow in NINE OF SPADES is in the warm yellows and oranges surrounding the dark blue and blue-green spades. Notice how the lighter blue-greens (turquoise) pave a way between these two value extremes in every feather. I was thinking that glittering yarns would create sparkle. DEVICE ALERT!! As you can see, it creates no such effect. Like a painter, I now use color to create these glimmers and shimmers instead of man-made metallics.

102 | *The Color Lab*

IN A WORD shows three poppies all glowing at different degrees. One is quite dull, possessing only two colors with a dull center, but shimmering a bit as it is warm against cool. The next is slightly more glowing; it has more sparkling places, uses more colors, and is properly shaded, with dark parts in the petals. Its center is a little more dynamic, incorporating different colors. The last, partially shown poppy is radiant. This poppy has more of all things color; it has more value range and more hues, which creates more glow. The fern frond's leaves glimmer quietly along their length.

This little *BRUCE PENINSULA* vignette, only 4" x 6", has lovely areas of glow. Light sparkles in the shallow water, rocks blaze in the sunlight, and the sky holds lovely glimmer. This is scrappy-strip hooking.

In my rug *DEARLY BELOVED*, this detail shows there is minimum value glow in this delphinium. With neither light nor dark present, they are dimmer than one might wish from a glowing area. I used a poorly dyed middle-value swatch. I added some darker values to the bottom but did not go far enough to create good glow. Prodding desperately calls out to be exaggerated in hue and value. Something about its sculptural quality demands it.

Creating Glow | 103

CREATING GLOW

Do you want some glow in your sky or in any rug? It is easy to do. All I did for SPIRIT OWL was find a plaid that had the color of my sky in it, as well as some yellow sections.

I cut the plaid and sorted the colors of the strips. I reserved the strips with yellow in one pile and the lighter green in another. I hooked all the lighter green next to the green background, and then used the yellow strips all in one centralized spot.

This worked well: it doesn't upstage my owl or my tree, and it creates another quiet area of interest.

CHOOSE THE AREA YOU WANT TO GLEAM OR GLOW

Every type of pattern can have some glow. It is best if this appears to occur naturally.

- Picture a woman with a beautiful glow about her; she appears not to have a scrap of makeup on but seems lit from within. That's what we want to emulate.

- In a landscape, look for the light source and where that light might shine—these are potential glows spots.

- In other rugs, we might shine in centers or on edges of motifs, as in geometrics. I'm lumping Oriental rugs and crewel-work styles into this category too.

- In portraits, determine the source of light shining in our visual aid.

- Study your patterns or visuals for the most natural areas to glow.

- Don't make glow appear on the right of most motifs and suddenly switch to the left side of others. The trick of glow is to replicate nature, to follow the line of light; light shines in a perfectly straight line, very predictably.

» ### GLOWING TIPS

- Achieve glow in smooth steps. Don't skip too many values. Creating a sharp-edged light patch in a dark area is not glowing, it is a klieg light!

- Using temperature to create glow means using warm colors to shine among cool ones. Remember, orange is the warmest color, blue the coolest. Any color around orange can glow.

- To make saturation glow, surround bright colors with dull colors.

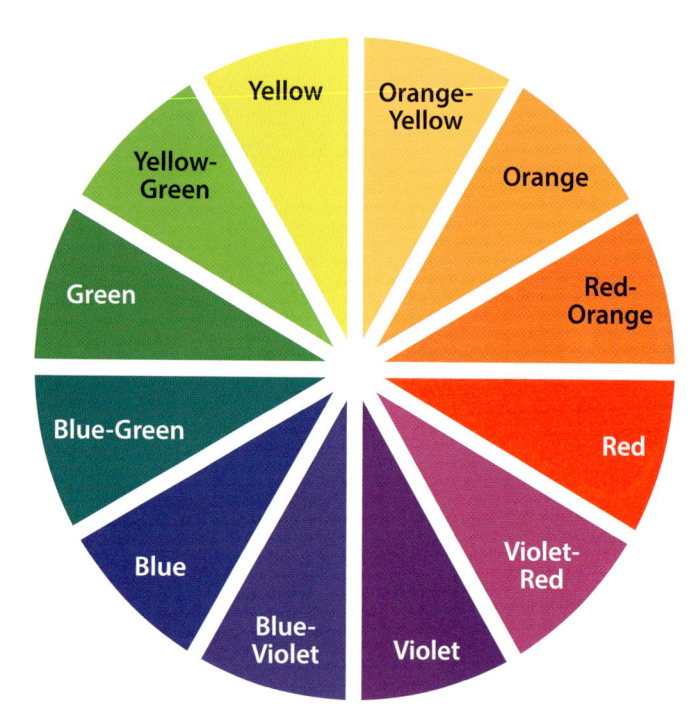

Look, a different color wheel! It will also do the job of helping us understand color relationships.

A GLOWING EXAMPLE

Let's try this out in theory. I have a purple sky, and I want glow. Which purple is my sky? Is the purple blue-violet, violet, or red-violet? The glow you choose will need to suit your project.

- Let's say it is blue-violet. I can use a lighter version of this color to glow. This is using value to glow. This can be dull or bright; saturation doesn't matter in this circumstance. Do what suits your rug.

- Or I can use a bit of violet. This is using temperature glow. Violet is a warmer color than blue-violet. I could choose a brighter version of the blue-violet in the same value. Or I could add a brighter version of blue-violet of the same value as the background to add some subtle glow.

Ok, I said a lot of palaver that perhaps made your eyes glaze over. Trust your instincts. You know when something is glowing. If you don't feel you know, try removing yourself a bit. Go back a distance to see if it is happening. Back up from these examples and take a look at them from afar.

HOOK A GLOW

It's time for action. You know what? You can make glow without hooking a loop. Just lay out wool in glowing arrays. Try it out, and then take a look at your gradations. Are they doing pretty work? If some areas are ugly, try another piece of wool. Smooth your steps; be subtler with your choices. It is important to be a smooth operator to achieve glow.

Here are some fun glow spots. On the top row, left to right, saturation is creating a very subtle glow. Next, we are traveling by hue from yellow to blue. This naturally goes from warm to cool and light to dark. The next one travels from orange to blue, going through violets. On the bottom row, we have a value glow. Next, a saturation glow; so quiet, but it makes an interesting comment on yellow-green, the notorious party girl. Then we have a hue glow. Hmmm . . . where is the glow appearing in this electric nipple? It is not exactly in the center. This treatment might be effective in certain things, like a leaf or a flower, or maybe in a sunset sky with lots of clouds. Those clouds are quite dark against the glow of the sky.

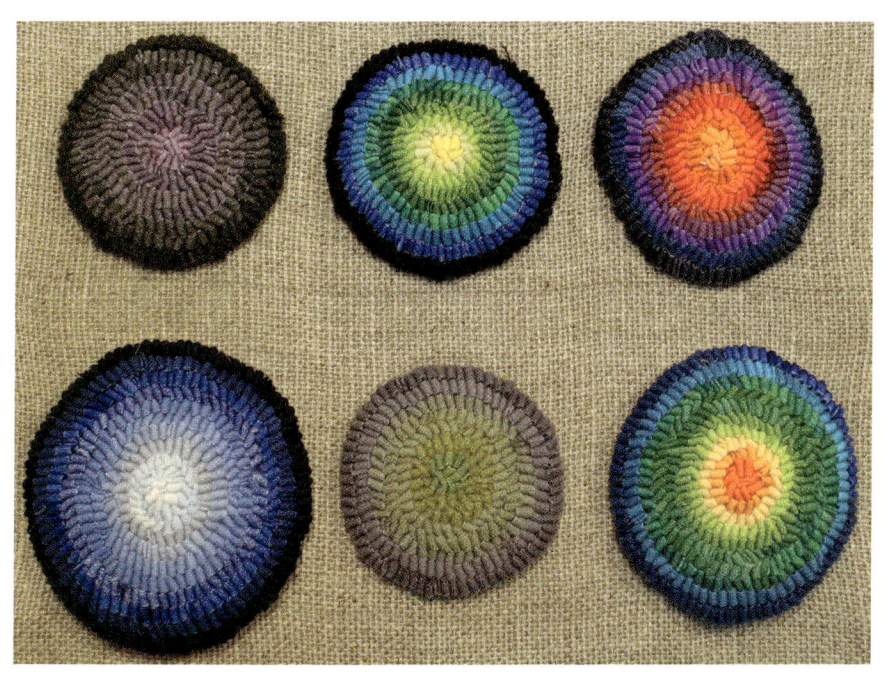

Look, I played a trick! I wanted to show you how glow is diminished when dark is not present. In the top photo, the glow spots have no dark outline. In the bottom photo, I hooked a dark ring around most of the glow spots. That dark line makes quite a difference.

Creating Glow | 105

Here is *September* again. We know red is a rather dark color. But there is glow in the background. I used the color device of three red stripes. The lighter, brighter, warmer red; a darker, cooler red; and a dull, warm, brownish red. Used together, the lighter red glows. But the main glow is coming from the lighter blue-greens and yellow-greens in the circles—they really shine. I used long strips that change color and go from light to dark. This increases their glow factor.

106 | *The Color Lab*

LAB WORK

MAKE SOME GLOW SPOTS

Make some of these glow spots. Just use the scraps that you have by now carefully sorted by color. I recommend starting with a value glow. If you are a beginner at glowing, you may find this the easiest glowing effect to try.

STEPS TO ADD GLOW

1. Look at the color you are working with where you want glow to appear.

2. Decide which component of color you will use to make glow, keeping in mind that if you don't have dark present somewhere in your piece, your glow will be diminished. Sometimes all three components will happen, as in SPIRIT OWL. I used yellow, a naturally light color that is warmer and brighter than the area surrounding it.

   - Value—make your color choice lighter
   - Saturation—make your color choice brighter
   - Temperature—make your color choice warmer

3. Create some color sketches or color plans to work out how this will happen in your project. Lay out wool in glowing arrays to make sure they flow smoothly.

4. Apply it. Try creating some glowing dots to practice this concept.

THINGS TO HANKER AFTER

- Seek out glow in other artwork and study how it came about through color work.
- Recognize the need for glow in your work.
- Understand that glow is one way to achieve more artistry in your work.
- Try to glow in the ways I've described using color.
- Recognize that glow happens more emphatically when dark is present.
- Give glowing a whirl.

10. CREATING DEPTH

Depth is a lovely tool to acquire. Creating depth depends on understanding the relationships of layers: what's on top or close, what is behind or far away, and what is between those two layers. Color applied to these layers is the way we explain to onlookers how far-reaching their view is, how deep their vista. These layers are also called planes, and they have behavioral traits or rules, if you will.

It is easy to use landscapes as an example of depth.

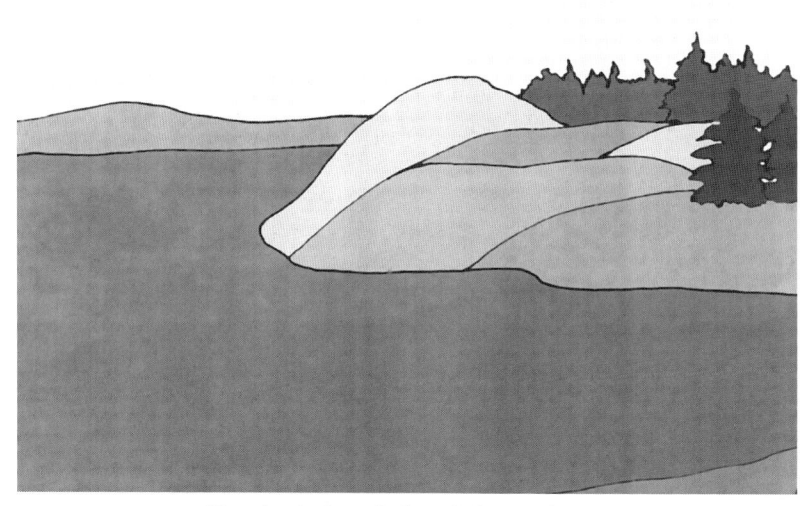

The simplest rendering of picture planes

Here is a little explanation of the planes and what they do colorwise:

Plane #1, the area closest to the viewer, should contain a lot of color details, higher contrast, and texture, and should have a lot of the darkest values or lighter values ones (or both) present. It is the boldest color layer.

Plane #2 will have less of what makes up Plane #1. The sizes of motifs will shrink a little, and the colors will dull or diminish.

Sometimes planes have two close objects, like trees, one behind the other on the same plane. We can treat these layered trees like a mini-plane and make the front tree a little lighter, brighter, and warmer than the one behind it. We are using the power of our color knowledge to draw this nearer tree forward.

Trees or anything tall are special. Sometimes they will be present through several planes, so using a darker value can help them stand out all along their length through many planes. The tallest of trees will most often be placed in the first or second planes, so using a darker value will keep these trees congruent throughout their length. That leads to good contrast.

Plane #3 will have even duller and lighter colors and less detail than Plane #2. Now, if you are short on values, this can get tricky. In the middle planes, we must be careful to have distinction. Remember that sometimes separation by one value is not enough, and we might need the separation of two values. We always want strong values when rendering a good depth of field.

If a picture is complex, it might have many layers or planes.

This dulling and lightening continues until we get to the infinite plane—the sky. The sky is a place where things can be brought back into the realm of brighter color, as in a sunset. It can have movement as well, such as scudding clouds or rain. Be careful to have it appear to sink back into the distance. Let it be the sky! This means it should be infinite, and not look flat like a wall. You want to imply it's arching above you. It must move into the distance at its bottom. Remember, the sky always illuminates the scene if the scene is in the daytime. Lighten and brighten it more than you think you should. It helps if you observe and follow the natural world; the sky is most often lighter at the horizon line and darkens slowly as more of it appears in the picture. (Of course, there are always exceptions to this rule, such as heavy weather or cloud cover.)

Sometimes, we have an object in a rug, like a rope on a swing, that will run through several differently colored planes. This rope will need to change values to remain looking like a whole length of rope and not disappear somewhere along the length of it. Again, making it dark might be the best bet. Here is an example in one of my own rugs.

I used a Greek letter phi to represent the golden mean in my journal rug, CIRCLE OF LIFE. It lies on two values of background. In order to give this letter a sense of wholeness, of being one and having both sides of the letter look the same value, I must use a hue of darker value and duller saturation on the right side.

Creating Depth | 109

DEPTH IN LANDSCAPES

This rug shows layers in a landscape. The perspective is that I'm in a canoe on the water, looking toward the shore line.

This little Spry Lake landscape is called *News from the Canoe*, 4" x 6", various cuts and materials on rug warp. Designed and hooked by Wanda Kerr, Wiarton, Ontario.

In order to examine the planes present in this landscape, let's divide the height into four 1" sections.

- Plane #1. The bottom inch is the first plane. It shows the water closest to the canoe. The water has lots of rich color, both warm and cool, light and dark.

- Plane #2. In the next inch, the second plane, the water is a little farther away, so it begins to act like a mirror to the sky. Some shadowing of the trees appears.

- Plane #3. The third inch, the next plane, is mostly shoreline and land, which is filled with trees in silhouette, backlit by the sunset. We see here some very dark colors. As the shoreline recedes from us, it becomes lighter and duller. The tree line reduces in height. This vista is rather short in length; we do not see the usual lightening and dulling of colors because of the time of day and the short depth of field.

- Plane #4. In the last inch, we have the infinity plane: a sky, as we know, stretches forever. That party girl, red-violet, right on top of the tree line, creates a big impact. The sunset is the reason we are looking at this view. All the other planes lead up to this one. As the sky rises up, it slowly fades to white, and then the violet evening sky starts to weigh in.

I carefully studied a photo to make this hooked landscape. Don't make a landscape up if you want a great one. Using a photo for a visual aid shows us the planes, the colors in them, the way the light falls, and what nature places in a plane to create depth. The stuff we might never dream of becomes very apparent with vigilant study. I always tell my landscape classes, "People, we cannot make this 'ahem' stuff up."

DEPTH IN PORTRAITS

We need to create the same depth of field in portraits. For me, a portrait is a landscape. Every portrait will have the hill of a nose, the cliff of a forehead, the plain of the cheeks, the cave of mouth and eyes, the more distant erratic rocks of the ears, the forest of hair. It is all there and can be treated very similarly. We have all seen portraits where everything is there that should be, but somehow it lies flat.

Start looking for planes, my friends; they are the secret of depth. Use color to help the first plane draw close and the last one move away.

CREATING DEPTH IN YOUR RUGS

You might not want depth in your rugs; that's up to you. I do. When looking at any realistic rug I make, I want viewers to feel that they can walk right into the scene, that they can step up and stand behind the subject or feel as though a bird might fly through the air at any minute. As a matter of fact, I call this ability to create depth "catching air."

If you want to catch air, you need to build yourself a bigger stash of wool. You need more brights and dulls and values. You need to be a better observer, to stop listening to crazy talk about how we should hook things, and look at them instead. Nature shows us all the rules for catching air. Do we not see everything every day and night of our lives in 3-D? It is all there for us to study. Take the time to look. Once you have the variety of wool you need and you can observe with understanding, you'll be "airborne"!

The subject of depth is so deep I could write a whole book about it. This is a terrible pun, but it is true. I've only touched on the basics here. If you study them, they will help you use color to relate space to your work. Using color effectively is how you do it.

When I teach depth of field, we work on little landscapes. I provide a full bag of cut wool, yarns, and trims—really, anything that can be hooked. If the goods are hookable, they are thrown in. Of course, it never matters what our loops are made of. What matters is the color of the materials, what we see in the loop tops. I supply way more hookables than needed so that students can make choices and the results will not be similar. I also supply way less of any one color that students are comfortable with so they learn to blend.

I don't discuss the parts of the picture: the water, sky, rocks, shore, trees or houses in it. We cannot see these as important if we want depth. They are all just parts of each plane.

We build our landscape from the first plane to the last. We make each plane section accurate to itself, and then add each subsequent plane with equal accuracy. Each step draws us back toward the sky.

If you can follow this premise, I guarantee you success in creating depth. Look out for the quagmire of your proclivities and predilections too. They will hang you up every time.

THINGS TO HANKER AFTER

- Start seeing planes as more important than specific parts of any realistic three-dimensional object or scene.

- Get a generous stash of color. You don't need much of any one color, you just need lots of values and saturations. (You can see how you might want to learn to dye, right?) Remember that you can use any loopable material to hook with. That opens up stash-enhancing opportunities a great deal.

- Start looking carefully at photos and scenes, people and things, for clues to catching air.

- Replicate photos by hooking them. Notice and edit out unimportant parts. Focus on the important color messages to re-create reality and to re-create depth.

- Understand that the more you focus on "parts," the less real your picture will be.

11. COLOR Q&A

I KNOW THE COLOR IS WRONG, BUT I CAN'T FIX IT!

Here are the things I do:

- Look carefully at the rug to determine if it is a value problem.

    - Do you have some extremes of light or dark in the rug?

    - Do things blend or stand out too much?

- Contrast is so important to create a beautiful rug. Remember to seek balance.

- Do you have a saturation problem?

    - How have bright or dull colors been placed?

    - Do they allow for a leading lady, something to focus on? Have you allowed "her stage" to be less important than she is?

- Is it a temperature problem?

    - Do you need a cooler or warmer yellow, red, blue, green, brown, orange, etc?

    - Do you have temperature balance?

Once you know what's wrong, address the problem. If you think you have more than one issue, start by looking at the colors, then the values, and then proceed to temperature, and finally, address saturation.

HOW DO I LEARN MORE ABOUT VALUES?

In each section of this book there are exercises to help you hook with more color knowledge. Some things can be head knowledge; others, like color use, must be heart-and-soul knowledge. We all move toward deeper knowledge by doing. Please do these exercises. It will open a whole new world.

WHY DON'T MY COLORS LOOK GOOD TOGETHER?

You might not have picked the color that will cover the greatest area first (usually the background). If you do this, you can play colors off that first pick and proceed, knowing they work together and with the leading lady.

- Stick to a theme. If your colors are Caribbean, stick with those colors. If you are working a Victorian vibe, always choose new colors from that theme's color palette. Don't throw something crazy in, and that includes poison.

- Be mindful of the use of poison. Don't use the same poison in the Victorian palette as the Caribbean one. Each theme will have a special color that sparks it. Poison is not only one or two colors. Poison is a small amount of bold color that vivifies the other colors you have used. What color poison you use will change with your theme. Feel free to be artful and whimsical, but look out for ugly.

- The answer you seek is probably staring at you in colors you've already hooked. A problem area can often be mended by using a lighter or brighter, darker or duller, warmer or cooler version of one of these colors.

- Remember, your leading lady is the most important player. Shine her up and let the rest of the colors support her.

- Beware of the domino effect. Change too many things, and you may lose your original color theme.

MY RUG LOOKS BLAH

- Did you pay attention to color temperature? It is important to balance temperature. A rug with all cool colors lacks heart and passion; one that's all hot will burn your eyes! You need the sweet relief of a cool color and the vivacity of a hot one.

- Do you have a balance of light, dark and medium values? Yes, this is all important! Don't be afraid to use extremes of value or saturation. And I beg you, please put your rug first. You may need to use a color you don't care for, but it may the one your rug cries out for. Be your rug's champion.

HOW DO I CHOOSE THE RIGHT BACKGROUND?

It works best to build the rug plan from the area that covers the most real estate first. Set the stage with that. Know it all: the value, the color, the texture or mix of colors, the temperature, and the saturation. This will set you free to build a great color plan.

- Look at what you want to convey. Textures will give a softer-edged look to your motifs. A solid single color creates a harder edge.

- Ask yourself, "Do I want my colors to shine or to be subdued? Do I want the edges of my motifs to melt into the background? Do I want the background to set a solid guard on my designs?"

- Test out your wools to see how they look with various backgrounds.

WHY DOES MY BACKGROUND LOOK STRIPY OR WORMY?

This is a value problem. Remove the darkest or lightest values. Replace them with neighboring colors of the same value.

WHAT CAN I DO IF I'M STUCK IN MIDDLE-VALUE HELL?

Stop buying wool. You can't trust yourself NOT to buy or dye middle values.

- Look for inspirations in artwork that use a wide variety of values. Get comfortable looking at contrasts.

- Next, get yourself some value tools as outlined in the value chapter. Use them on your stash to determine what you are missing. Put those values in your wallet to pull out as a list of sorts to throw down on any wool you might spy. Now you can buy wool or dye again, but only those values you don't have.

- It is a very common problem. I say this as diplomatically as I can, but I'm shouting: 95% of the wool for sale is in the middle values, so LOOK OUT! You will want it, but remember, hue is not as important as value is in the building of beautiful rugs. Save yourself!

HOW DO I PREDICT COLOR INTERACTION IN A COLOR PLAN?

Try hooking the colors up against each other the way they will be used. I don't find making a roll of wool very informative. Once, I hooked a value scale of all the colors I used in a portrait. I was pleased to see, in the context of value, they did not look like themselves as they appeared on the shelf or as they looked hooked in the rug. Instead they became one with the value scale and changed appearances like a secret agent in disguise.

If you know your work will have magenta against teal, hook a few rows of these together to test their worthiness. You might find you need to dull your magenta or pop up the teal, to make it more pleasing. Rug hookers need to adopt the practice so many other crafters use: do tests or little mock-ups for possible color interactions. Let's get on that!

I WOULD LIKE TO COMBINE WARM AND COOL COLORS, BUT I DON'T KNOW HOW.

The best way to do this is by working a transitional color between them. You can read more about this in Chapter 8, Creating Transitions.

- You can keep a commonality between them, like using the same value and saturation.

- Colors directly opposite each other (complementary colors), will jangle. Seek a dull color or two between them on the color wheel, and insert these between the janglers to smooth the flow.

I HAVE A LOT OF GREENS, ALL THE GREENS GOING, IN A HOOKED PIECE I'M WORKING ON. HOW CAN I HAVE THEM ALL SHOW UP?

You need contrast. Look to hue, value, saturation, and temperature to make these greens work for you. Things close up will be lighter, or darker, or both. This is an area of extremes. The greens will be more saturated here and be warmer.

As you move away, use the greens that are medium valued and reduced in saturation. You will stop using the warmer yellow-greens and begin to use wools that are truer green with some blue-green. As you move into the distance, the greens should become duller, lighter, and cooler.

HOW CAN I USE INTERESTING UNEXPECTED COLORS TO CREATE A FAUVIST LOOK IN MY WORK?

Every color has a value, including realistic ones. A different, wilder color can pinch-hit for a realistic color if:

- it is the same temperature,

- it has the same saturation (unless you want to heighten that over the whole design),

- or the color is the same value as the one you are replacing. This is the most important factor.

- I liken this to playing a song you know in a new key.

The Fauvists are a group of artists who used very expressive, unrealistic colors for their artwork of real objects. I call this using the spiritual colors of a person, place, or thing.

WHILE USING MULTIPLE COLORS FOR A MORE PAINTERLY EFFECT TO CREATE A SECTION OF A MAT THAT I WANT TO READ A CERTAIN COLOR (LIKE NAVY), HOW DO I PICK THE OTHER COLORS TO COMBINE TO READ THAT COLOR?

Find the color family or the hue you want to be primary. For this example, we'll choose dark blue. Look on either side of it. Those are the colors to use: green, blue-green, blue-violet, blue—even red has a place if the red is dull. If red is placed beside green, it will make a dark little jangle. If you put purple between them, the jangle will be quieted. For the best effect, the colors all must have the same value and saturation. You'll get some good optical blending, great merriment, and, up close, a wonderful surprise.

I WANT HARD AND FAST RULES ON COLOR USE.

My dear sweet thing, would it be that all of life is this way, but it isn't. Nope. Because every color is affected by every other color, there can be no rules without exceptions, and the exceptions are legion. I've found hidebound thinking about color use creates the biggest of rug problems out there.

I'm still battling against false color rules and statements made before I was born. The best thing to remember, if you need a rule, is that are there are no rules. There is only a color—a color working very well or a color not working at all. You are going to have to be more adventuresome, analytical, and inventive. Be brave and try things out.

I HAVE A TERRIBLE TIME MAKING DECISIONS ABOUT COLORS.

All colors have special friends who make them look amazing. There are billions of choices. Try not to settle too quickly when you are planning with colors. There is always a good-better-best scenario.

I spend a lot of time working and playing with color. Get yourself some colored toys like pencils, markers, paints, crayons, yarns—whatever you feel comfortable with. No one needs to see you playing or judge these experiments. I like paint chips to mix and match and explore with. Look at layouts in expensive magazines, on fabric, or on websites to see effective and non-effective color interplay. Figure out what colors you like, then look at the different variations in that color family for inspiration.

Look around you. Be a student of nature—the best and most balanced use of color is outside! I cannot stress enough to PLAY, PLAY, PLAY with color every day to gain confidence and inspiration.

> "But having had your bright, fresh, original idea, the really hard part is turning it into a successful product. That's what takes all the sweat."
>
> — TREVOR BAYLIS, ENGLISH INVENTOR OF THE WIND-UP RADIO

CRITIQUING YOUR WORK

Part of learning good color use is the art of the beady-eyed look, the tearing off of your romantic, rose-colored glasses to see what you have not yet seen. Learn to look sharply.

Look at your work from a distance of 8 feet or more, as though you are seeing it for the first time. I mount my rug on a wall and walk out of the room. A few minutes later, I walk in with my mind clear and clean of any notions I have about this rug. I look carefully and listen closely to it.

1. Do your main motifs attract attention immediately?
2. Are things showing up as what they are: does a rock look like a rock? Can they be read as such by most viewers? Ask a kid to tell you about the rug if you want to know if things look as they should.
3. Are things blending where they ought to?
4. Is there contrast where it is needed?
5. Have any inadvertent shapes been created in backgrounds or features that are distracting or suggestive of something else you don't want to show the world?
6. Does something steal attention away from your main feature?
7. Are you in love with an idea or action (like using ribbons or underpants to hook with) or what you imagine you are seeing but no one else can make it out? Is there something in your rug that you might be romantically attached to but it just isn't working?

Pertaining to landscapes or portraits specifically:

1. Are your dark areas dark enough?
2. Are the light areas light enough?
3. Is your water a complete and good mirror of your sky? Are the eyes a good mirror of the soul?
4. Do your color temperatures jive together?
5. Do you have glow? Could you have more glow through wider value contrast?
6. Do you have sight lines that drop off, don't connect, or end mysteriously?
7. Is value placement congruent with the light source?
8. Does your sky illuminate? Is the skin alive with glow?

I learn what I need to know by looking and asking myself these hard questions. Once you answer these questions, you can decide to do whatever you want with the information, including nothing.

The next time you plan a hooking project, remember what you might have changed with the last few rugs. When these questions are applied, each work is an opportunity for greater works in the future. These questions can be applied to any project.

Detail of *September*. See the full rug on page 106.

Color Q & A

Hints for Color Use in Rug Hooking

- A light or pale color area surrounded by a dark one looks bigger than a dark color area surrounded by a pale one.

- Light backgrounds "steal" color saturation away from motifs, making them appear smaller and receding.

- Dark backgrounds enhance color saturation and make them advance to the eye.

- If you use a medium-colored background, make sure all parts of the motifs are at least three values lighter or darker.

- Colors indicate moods. They have emotional attachments and meanings; use this to your advantage.

- Every color has a value. Use a digital camera set to black and white to help you see value. Trust your naked eye too; not all value-finding devices are equally refined.

- Create contrast. Don't be afraid to use a big value jump between two colors if it suits what you are building.

- Embrace using dark values. They provide depth and let other colors glow.

- Think of the colors chosen for rugs as your palette. Make sure the palette "belongs to a theme" and that all parts suit one another.

- Your palette is chosen and you have begun hooking. Suddenly you run into a problem. Revert to your original palette for answers. The best answer already lies in your rug and the colors you have already used. Go for a darker or lighter value of one of the chosen colors, if none of the original materials will work. Next try a duller or brighter version, if value fails to remedy your problem.

- Recognize that although blue and purple usually make excellent partners, not every blue looks good with every purple. The same goes for every other color combo.

- As you create your palette, think of the good-better-best scenario.

- When color planning, start with a color you love. Use it in a large area. Find supporting colors that enhance it or are enhanced by it.

- Choosing your background color first is key: not just whether it will be light or dark. You will see how colors react and play off one another and save yourself hours and days of bothersome replacing.

- Maintain a color theme, i.e., Egyptian, Santa Fe, ocean, Victorian. For instance, make sure the blue you use is the blue for your theme, and the yellow, and the orange, and so forth.

- No color stands alone; colors are completely influenced by the surrounding colors. This is why it is important to consider all colors in a rug at once.

"... Feel your own creative force, your own inventive spirit."

- A color you don't like may enhance the one you love.

- The temperature of any given color can change according to the surrounding colors. A warm yellow-green may look cool if surrounded by hot orange, red, and yellow.

- Color is all around us, and we so seldom see it fully. Become color aware; it will help your eye to glean more information, and it is the visual equivalent to stopping and smelling the roses. So, take a peaceful moment, observe, and notice the wisdom of nature's color array.

- The best tool you can have is a good friend you can trust to tell it like it is. It is difficult for anyone to look at their hooking work with a fresh view. No one is exempt from this myopia.

- Combine colors we don't think of as usually working well together, such as red and green, by playing with the size of the colors, their values and saturations.

- If you ask for color advice, don't let your adviser railroad your original intention.

- If you need color help or wool, take your rug and all the wool being used when you go shopping so the salesperson can offer you skillful, well-informed help.

- Use paint chips, fabrics, or other tools to communicate effectively with others about color. We are not all created equal in our ability to "see" colors. We talk about them as if everyone knows exactly what we mean by burnt orange or brick red or navy blue. We are each unique, thanks to the rods and cones in our eyes.

- Don't forget about the very useful neutrals. If they are used well, they provide a delicious setting for our "diamonds" or flashier colors.

- If you find your rug unpleasant to look at, perhaps two strong colors are having a turf war. Make one color area smaller than the other.

- Textures, spot dyes, and plaids are often difficult to use while looking for good contrast. This is because they often contain many colors.

- If adjacent areas of hooked textures share a single color in common, optical blending occurs where they meet in a motif. This blurring of your motif and background creates a very a soft-edged contrast.

- Textures, plaids, and spot dyes all have values. Read the values by hooking up a sample and using our value-finding tools.

- Colors can be described as light or heavy, soft or hard.

- Color plans are not written in stone, but be wary of making too many changes to a plan. This can result in a domino effect of descending chaos.

> "Color is a beautiful tool that can work as a hammer or a feather, as chocolate or lemon, as a toddler or a ballerina."

COLOR PLANNING 101

There are two types of planning. You can make up a color plan. Or you can use a visual aid, and through carefully studying and closely following it, discover the colors present in it. I've covered that technique in the Chapter 6.

MAKING UP A COLOR PLAN

First pick a theme to give you direction. This can be anything that makes you think of color, like market day, Santa Fe, Biscayne Bay, fall forest walk. You could think about a county cabin, a beach house, a castle, a city loft.

It helps to think of themes that you are familiar with and already love. Your Joy Book could really help you; those pages you love are filled with carefully crafted color combinations. A theme will help you pick out initial color-wheel colors.

But beware: you need to pay attention to the colors you are selecting. It can't be just any yellow. It must be the right yellow, the right value, the right temperature, close to the right saturation. Too many near-misses of color selection will veer you right off your theme's track.

> "Don't go in for the "yellowish" if what you need is "yellow."
> Never settle for less; Go for the exact thing!"
>
> —Israelmore Ayivor, inspirational writer

This is damn hard for me to simplify because my working motto is *anything can be any color!* Can you feel my pain? But for your sake, I'm going to talk about the fall forest walk theme. In this theme, we know we will have a plethora of warm colors. And we are not likely to use bright violet or light violet. But we could punch up our yellows by using grayed-out violet in our sky's clouds or in our tree trunks. If we dominated our forest with orange, it would behoove us to add blue-green where I would add violet. Do you see what I mean? I love to bite into the whole apple of color available to me. But let's go back to you; I just wanted to show you the window of possibilities available.

- You need to pick out the color for the largest area. Make sure it is a color you don't mind looking at, because you will be hooking a lot of it. Now, lay it out.

- Find the color for the next biggest area. Balance it to the background: warm against cool, bright against dull. Make these two colors several values apart.

- Audition it by laying it right on the stage of the background.

- Now make sure those two are talking beautifully between each other, make sure they are in LOVE. Keep laying down possibilities until you find deep love, not some sham or shifty love. There is too much sham love already in this world! This is the concept of good, better, best—try for the best!

- Now start laying down the smaller areas; again, look for the joy of true love. Some colors are tolerant of each other, while others are will interweave and dance like soul sisters and brothers. Look for the ignition of spirit.

- These smaller areas are often places where we can use more exciting color, the highly saturated bright colors. To choose those, we look at colors opposite to our main colors.

- While you are planning, look to include some very desaturated areas; we need a restful place.

- Now I can safely tell you (if you've read this book like a novel) it is time to use light, dark, bright, and dull because you now understand what that means! The middle of all these parts of color will carry you between the opposites. Look to see if now you need a few colors to link the ones you chose: do you need transitions between some colors?

- I'm not a fan of rolling up colors to see if they work together, because it discounts the amounts you will use, and this will affect the relationship greatly. Lay out the main colors in a space about the same size as they will appear in your rug and place the rest of the possible colors proportionally on top of them to get a feel for how colors will behave together.

- Play at color planning with your stash. Do this a couple of times a week for a month or so. Try planning by matching a visual—a card, or a basket of fruit or flowers. Try a rug pattern you have in your stash next.

- Use your camera: take a photo, then change it to black and white to check values. You will only learn to do this by doing it!

> "I am always doing what I can't do yet in order to learn how to do it"
>
> —Vincent van Gogh

INSPIRATION FOR COLORISTS

1. You are unique in this world; there is only one of you. Because of this, your inside rugs (like an inside voice) must be stunning. Please, let them out to play.

2. So . . . yeah, I know, I just wrote this book, but don't believe anything you read or hear about anything. Try it yourself. Does it work as stated? Great! No? Blow that off and move along to find a better way. There is so much misinformation out there that it's scary. Misinformation will impede your development and blossoming.

3. Look every dang place you can to find one soul who will be a stand-up guy and tell you that the face you just hooked looks like a frog. Hopefully, that guy will also stand up to aid you in learning how to pucker up, kiss that frog, and turn it into a prince.

4. Creativity, imagination, artistry, and inspiration all require your involvement, your work. Get involved with your soul. Turn the telescope around; instead of looking out there at others, look at your own magnificent self. You are divine, don't you know? An authentic action soars you up in the stratosphere. The action of copying another's soul drives you seven miles below ground.

5. You already have everything you need: all the books, the wool, the hooks, the backing, the ideas, the body, the desire, the willingness to put what you want up front on your schedule. If you don't have that yet, then get to it, my darlings. Go steady with yourself, take yourself on fantastic dates, lavish yourself with attention, get together and spend time with the one you love . . . you! Get you and your splendid desires together frequently. The clock is ticking on you and your dreams.

6. Organize: your wool, your studio, your house, your meals, your errands. Revamp with the thought of creating more downtime for yourself. If you do all your errands in one day, you will have more at-home time, which means more ruminating time, more peaceful and restorative times, and more delicious walking-about time. We are meant to walk and think at the same time. Wonderful things will happen if you let thoughts play out like each step follows the next. Get out of your funk. Get busy living the life you want. Never mind about dang Facebook. You are missing the life in front of your face! Tick, tick, tick.

7. Be nice, okay? Never mind about what other people are doing. What people think of you is none of your business—keep your nose to the loop.

8. Decision making is the bread and butter of making anything. Learn how to know what you want. Your rugs will improve and thank you for it! No shillyshallying.

9. Oh, you are going to make mistakes—lots of them. They are a bit of alchemic magic though, these mistakes, because out of the dross of disaster, you pull gold. You are learning.

10. Learning is important. It keeps us juicy and alive, and it keeps us sharp as we age. It is cumulative. Picture it as a treasure box. Every snippet we garner is stored to be used again. So often, in each class we take, we don't bring ahead what we have gathered in our box. Only learned-from-experience snippets go in your treasure box, not the learned-by-rote and know-in-your-head stuff. The colors you love to lean on, the shapes that bring you joy, the stories you have to tell, your wise ways with a texture—these are your treasure box goods.

Mic Mac, 43" x 24", #3- and 6-cut wool on burlap. Designed by House of Price and hooked by Wanda Kerr, Wiarton. Now that you have made it to the end of this book, study the color work in this rug. Notice the scroll transitions, notice the variation in the background. Imagine how much fun it was to hook this rug using all the elements of color. You too can do this with all your new color knowledge.

Color Q & A | **121**

12. COLOR CREATIVITY

YOUR COLOR CHOICES

This is a terrible way to start an encouragement chapter, because I don't want to nag or chastise you, but I'm going to anyway. Your proclivities can work for you or against you. They can create a sense of style for you; they ensure unique ways of using color that are your signature. They can also mire you down into a repeated pattern of color use that jails you and prevents you from fulfilling your promise as an artist.

Knowing your biases, knowing your patterns of thinking, learning, and ideas about color are the first steps toward realizing your potential. And you do have potential. The only thing standing between you and the engagement of your artistic sensibility is you.

So often we want the easy fix; we want to find our true mentor, the right teacher, the right book, the right class, or rug, or wool to learn what we want to know.

If you'll pardon this earthy comparison, wanting to be more creative and artistic is rather like having a baby. Conception is like the desire to be an artist. You already have everything you need right inside you. Instead of recognizing this, we run around looking for somebody else who has already had a baby to work this out for us. We want patterns, color plans, drawings, maps. We want this baby delivered to us already born, washed, dressed, wrapped, and handed over all pretty and tidy.

When we choose that path, it is harder to bond to our baby, or in other words, to our subject. We are missing the hard work of birthing, of creating. We are searching for surrogates who will give us a blue-eyed darling just like theirs.

If you want or need to have a surrogate, I'm all for that. We must work in a way our courage allows us to work at any given time. But this surrogacy creates an agency where you are coming in half or three quarters of the way through the process.

My skills are more in the midwife realm. I'll help you in any way I can. I'll be by your side helping you through your process, not doing it for you. I'll wipe your brow and your tears. I'll clean up your messes and set you to work again. I'll pace and listen and give you a tip or ten. I'll look way in to see how far you are along, because it can be difficult for you to tell, and it can be hard labor. You'll need encouragement. When the baby arrives, I'll be awestruck by the mightiness, by the gutsiness, by your bravery in giving birth to what you conceive. It is a moment as sacred and glorious as any other birth.

It won't be any part of me or mine; it will be all yours.

OWNING YOUR PROCESS IS KEY TO YOUR DEVELOPMENT

If you don't know you are a Sister of the Light, your work will suffer. For instance, when you hook that lighthouse, you will not want it to be in the dark. But this is what lighthouses are for, to shine a light in the dark. If you want to have a beacon alight, then it must include darkness to shine through.

If you only like blue in your work and refuse orange in any way, the color you love suffers. Including hated opposites is a chore if the color nearly makes us puke. If we can prevail, we are rewarded by our blues suddenly becoming richer and more glorious..

If you only buy or dye dull colors and one day want to create a landscape, you have only dull tools to create objects that are close. Your landscape will be as flat as a wall.

It's okay to have preferences and biases; we all do. But creating great works, those with excellent color use, means we must first know our biases and then be able to set them aside for the greater good of our projects.

Learn your biases, accept them, and take steps to overcome them.

LOOKING FOR INVENTIVE COLOR

Often it is hard to see exactly what is going on with visual aids. We assume that because our house is white or green or red, that is the color we must pick out to hook it. But our house is not a paint sample—it is a three-dimensional object in space with shadows and light effects from surroundings, weather, and time of day. Having a photo to study helps weed out our assumptions about what is going on and lets us process the relativity of the colors portrayed. This visual lets us relate more artistically to our inspiration. We see what else is present in our white, green, or red house by studying the colors found in each shadow, light area, trim edge, and window shine.

This idea works for everything we hook—even something as silly as a snowman! We know what a real snowman looks like in our mind's eye. When we come to hook it though, we need to exaggerate, to emphasize the snowman-ness of it, to expand and expound on the possibilities inherent in a snowman—the snowman's spirit.

Color is the vehicle for finding that spirit! This snowman defies what we know about a snowman. Our snowman is warm and cool. The snow in him is not white, the sky is not blue, and we know snow on the ground is not a violet texture. No matter how strange the colors used, we are seeing just what we need to. We are seeing a snowman in snow. It works.

Getting in touch with the more spiritual application of color can seem daunting. Thinking about colors and their meanings is a great starting point. Perhaps white is a sorrowful color for you, when black is the mourning color for everyone else. This is a key to exercising your own will and passion, your own spirit. There are many references available to use and explore these meanings for your edification. You'll find these in our references at the end of the book.

Doing the lab work in each chapter will help you discover your shortcomings. Once you work through those, you can really soar. Like most poker players, we have a "tell." You have a way of working that lets anyone know you are the creator. It is as good as a signature. Your "tell" might also create a recurring situation where, no matter the subject, you run into the same problem, rug after rug. It might be a lack of contrast, a repression of blue, too many warm colors, or no strong color theme. But your problem happens every time you are left to your own devices.

Wouldn't it be great to overcome this? Wouldn't it be wonderful to use color with intention? The lab work in each chapter will help you through this struggle. Now that you've read this far, go back and do the exercises in order. Set yourself free!

This is a part of the birthing process only you can do. Because of your unique view, makeup, and experiences, this work will be idiosyncratic, speaking directly of your individuality. Once you do the lab work set out in each chapter, you can better understand what I suggest.

LET'S BE FRIENDS, 18" x 28", #4- to 8-cut wool on linen. Designed and hooked by Wanda Kerr, Wiarton, Ontario.

MAKE A JOY BOOK

One of my Joy Journals

You need to start heeding your own color desires—and they might not be what you imagine. We can get stuck in a rut here just as we can in the rest of our lives.

Grab yourself a pile of beautiful magazines. Spend $50—it will be the best money you've ever spent! Only buy magazines you find delicious to riffle and flip through. With these, we will unlock your inner color lion.

Pull out each page that you love. If it is only a photo on that page, cut it out. Paste these into a scrapbook. This is like an old-school Pinterest board where you can collect all that you love to look at. Add some words to your pages and some paint chips you love. Glue some of your favorite wool samples to it.

You can use your Joy Journal to plumb designs for rugs. It will help you discover shapes and line forms, sizes, gradations; all the design elements you love will appear.

And for our purposes, it will indicate to you the most important element of design: COLOR! Here you will see the colors of your present and of your exciting color future. When you have 20 pages filled, take a look at them and relate them to our color families.

- Which colors appear most often?
- Which colors don't show up at all?
- Do black or white or gray appear?
- What values are there?
- What levels of saturation?
- What temperatures do you favor?
- How do these colors compare to your already hooked projects or wool stashes?

Plan a rug using this group of your very favorite colors derived from one of your visuals. The colors will be in perfect balance—the magazine world is highly contrived and designed.

Now, after what I just said about birthing, I'm giving you some patterns to play with to help firm up your labor muscles. If you are not familiar with putting pencil to paper, or marker to backing to draw your own pattern, you are climbing a steep enough hill looking at your color use without adding drawing into the mix. These patterns are yours to use as you wish for personal color study use. Adapt these aids as you wish.

Set out goals to try my color play lessons. Even if you feel you know quite a bit about any given subject, do the exercise anyway. You could be fooling yourself. I know I fool myself all the time, and there is nothing like having proof your brain is playing tricks.

Here are some tips for more creative color use:

- "Don't let the perfect be the enemy of the good." --Voltaire, French writer

- Anything can be any color.

- Look around, be a more careful observer.

- To use more artful colors to paint something in wool, seek out and use the neighboring colors of that object.

- Resistance is the first step in learning: feel it, look at it, toss it over your shoulder, and move ahead.

- It is important to lead with imagination (instead of relying on what we know).

- The experience of "bringing our skills" to a new idea is pivotal for growth. --Diane Ericson, designer and cloth artist

BUILD A GOOD WORKING STASH

I suggest you cull your stash and do something with good wool you don't really like. (But please look out for the urge to remove all the colors you don't like.) If you want the colors you love to sing, they need some of your uglies to do so. Felt this culled wool, dye it some color you need, or pass it on. Get rid of substandard goods. The stash that is cramped and largely invisible is not a good working stash.

You probably already have much of what you need. Depending on the "value club" you belong to, some of the good color bases are covered right now. That's a great start.

In a perfect world, I'd like you to have a color or colors from all the stations around the color wheel. I'd like you to have all nine values of most of the hues, plus white and black.

I'd like you to have some relative warm and cool versions of the color families you use most. I'd like you to have a good range of bright to dull. I'd also like you to have a good array of neutrals and warm and cool grays in most values.

Usually you don't need much of any one color for my "whole color use" work. It is easy to substitute colors that match in value and saturation. That expands your stash options handsomely.

If you dye, you can start filling in your hue and value gaps first. If you buy wool, you need a good shopping list of the values you need. Take a value scale and cut it up into sections. When you find out what you are missing, take those value chips with you so you can throw them down on wool you are courting to read its value before you buy.

Cut up a color wheel to carry as well, and take only those colors you need. Only buy colors in those families. This might be hard, but be strong!

Take your time building your stash. You can still get what appeals to you, but balance that out with what your "wool pantry" is missing.

To store your collections of smaller pieces of wool by color, buy large rings from a craft store and several 2" safety pins. Pin the wool pieces onto the rings so they slip around it easily; pin them according to value for the best access.

Storing wool by color on rings with safety pins; we call these passels. The wool was collect by Heather Burns and the passels were curated by Alicia Kay.

Color Creativity | **125**

PATTERNS FOR YOUR USE

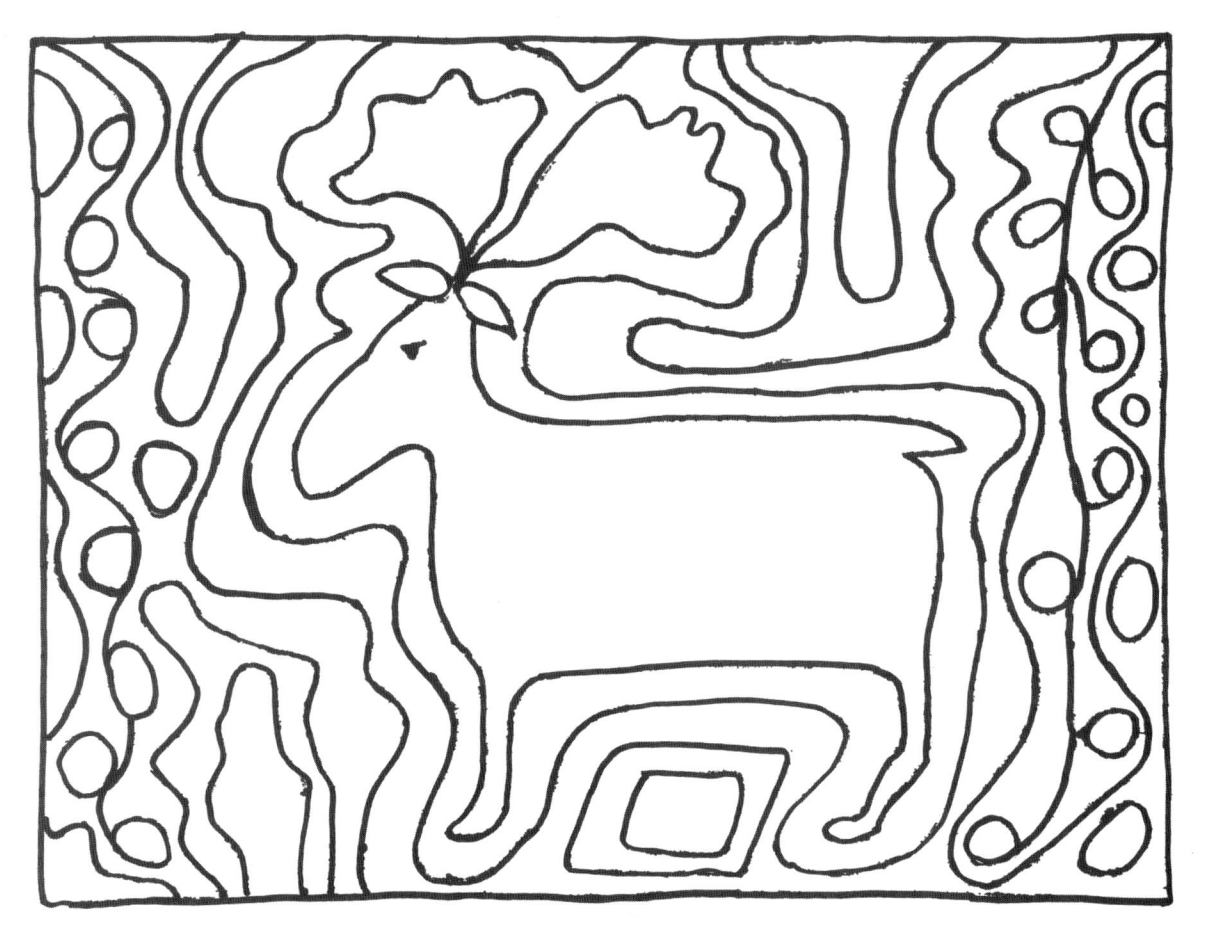

SPIRIT MOOSE. This pattern has plenty of stylized patterning to play with. Emphasizing color placement in different areas will make the area either the background or an important support actor for the moose.

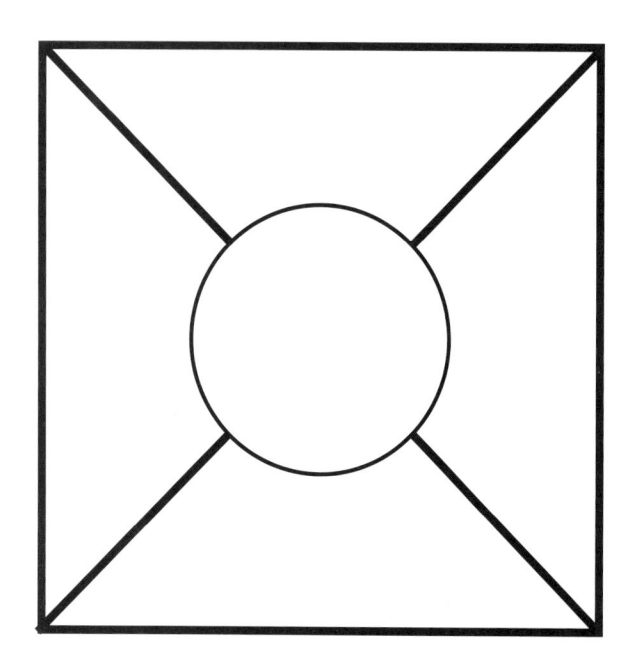

WOOLGATHERING CHALLENGE. See Julie's hooked rug on page 40.

In the pattern INTERSECTIONS, there are rows of goofy, irregular overlapping circles that do not intersect between rows. The goofy circles create good tension with their uneven edges and the shapes that are made when they overlap. There are repeats in this pattern, but they do not feel stiff or become monotonous to look at. The slightly different sizes carry interesting weights to different areas. Also, a necessary border band around the edge stops the madness, ceases the confusion. It is a little ugly in this form.

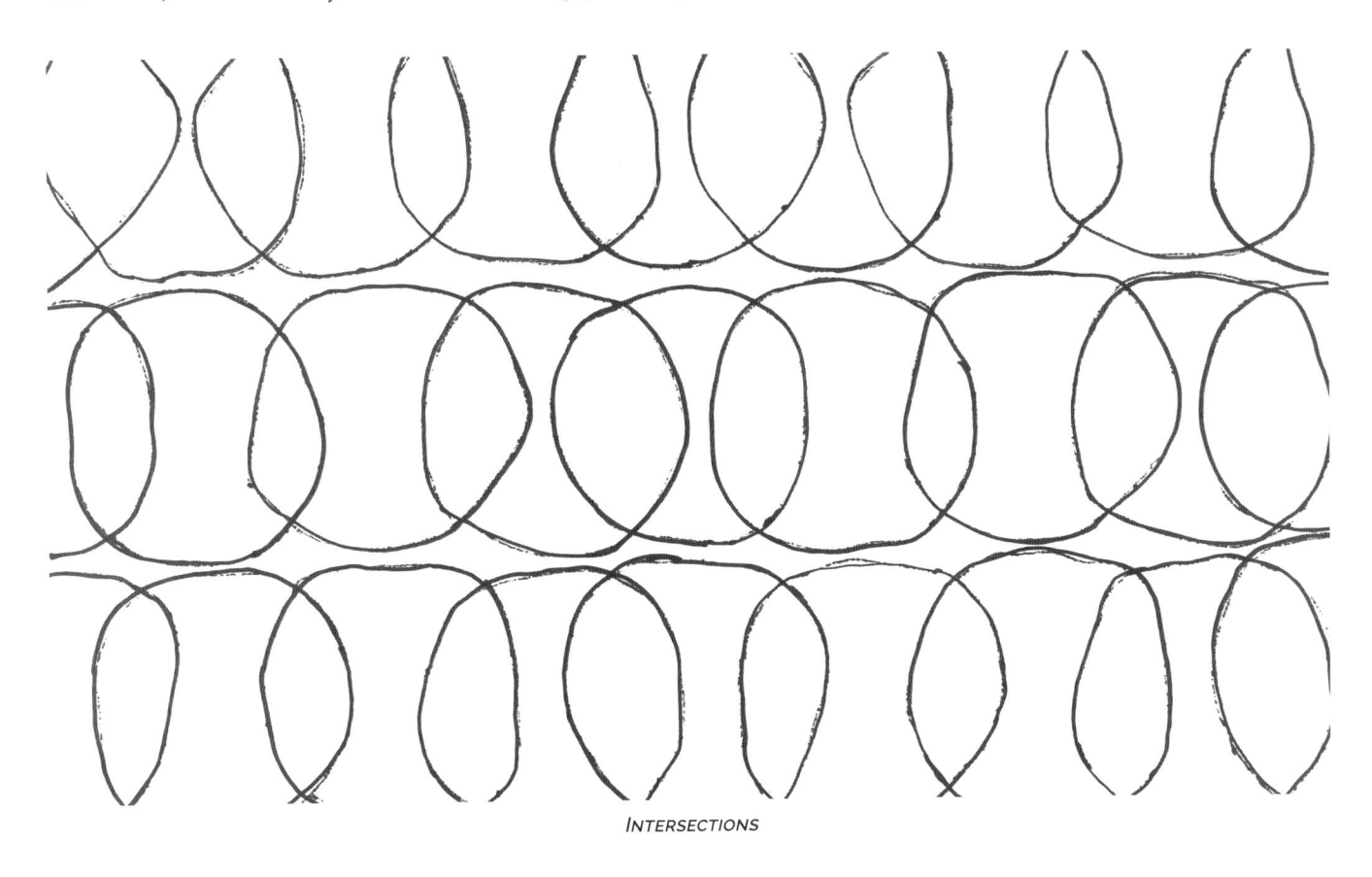

INTERSECTIONS

Here is how you make the INTERSECTIONS pattern. You can use my two circles if you wish or draw your own.

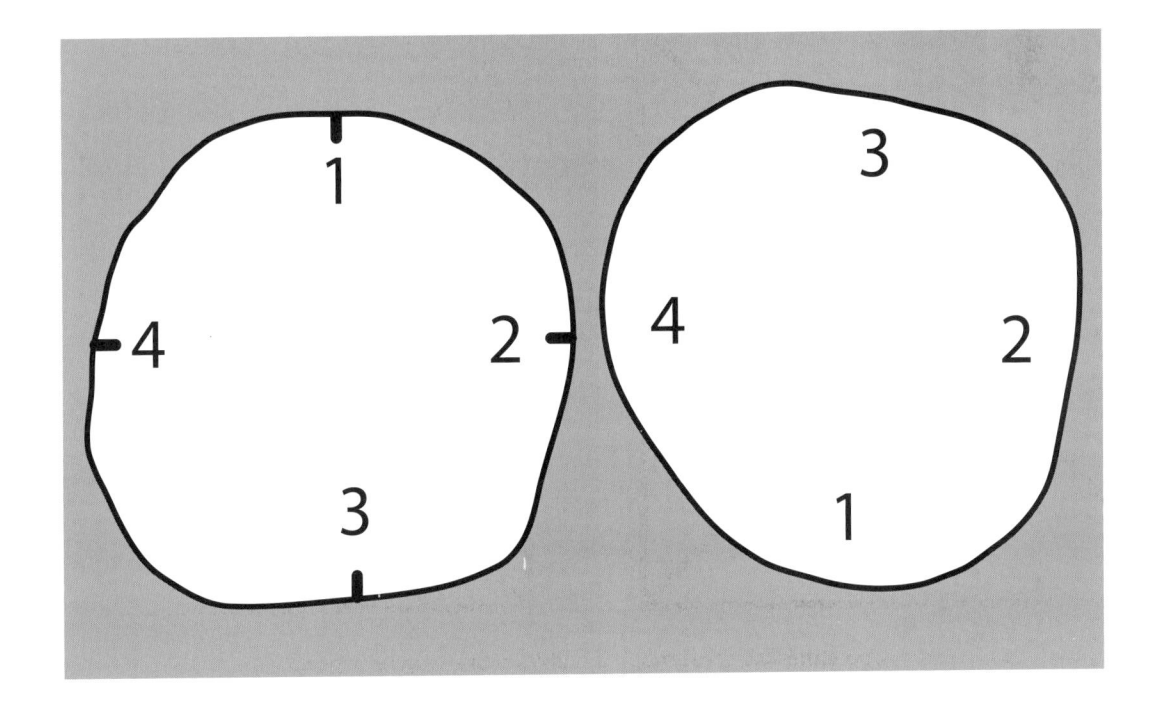

Color Creativity | **127**

First, I drew two circles that were oddly shaped. This was harder than it looks.

Next, I numbered them at quarter points so the overlapped shapes could vary. The overlapped shapes (intersections) are very important when we commence to color this piece.

When I drew the circles on my backing, I let two different numbers meet and overlap each time. There is a finite number of combinations—just enough to get a wonderful random appearance.

- Let #2 on one circle and #3 on the other meet to intersect.

- Then let #2 on one circle and #1 on the other meet to overlap.

- Next let #3 and #4 meet, and so on and so on.

To make sure everything looked as I wished, I drew it on paper first. I liked how the rows traveled off all four sides of the design, as if the color work continues on its path. This is a pleasing element to include in a design.

You can use this pattern to play with color in many ways.

- Say one circle is orange and the one beside it is blue; where they intersect will be a gray.

- Or you could play with values: one circle will be light and the other will be dark, so the intersection will be medium-valued.

- Or one could be warm and the other cool, and the intersection would be a neutral temperature (relatively speaking).

- Or you could make one bright and the one beside it dull, and the intersection between them will be neutrally saturated.

INTERSECTIONS, 24" x 18", #8-cut wool on linen. Designed and hooked by Wanda Kerr during her online class titled Spark, 2017.

128 | *The Color Lab*

CONCLUSION

Finally, I want to talk straight to you.

I want you to go beyond expected outcomes with your work, and I think you want that too. This means if you think you must follow certain truisms or dictates of rug hooking, try your best to lay them aside. Yes, you have to push away these old maps in order for something new to happen, for a new flight path to appear. I advise students not to look at already constructed rugs to see how they might go forward in their own way. To look at other rugs means you are only inspired to do the same or close to the same. You might feel the spirit of the person who made that piece by looking at it, but spirit cannot be gained by devouring their heart or by copying them. You are not hungry for what they are and what they created. You are hungry to feel the intensity of your own creative force, your own inventive spirit.

Now that's something toothsome to chew on.

A DEEP AND HEARTFELT THANK YOU TO EVERY PATIENT PERSON ON MY TEAM WHO BROUGHT THIS PROJECT TO FRUITION. I'M ALSO INCREDIBLY GRATEFUL FOR EACH OF MY STUDENTS WHO LED ME TO DEEPER UNDERSTANDING AND USE OF COLOR. BLESS YOU ALL.

REFERENCES

Unusual palettes:
The Designers Guide to Color Combinations, by Leslie Carbarga (North Light Books, 1999)

To find new, unusual palettes, try this book. It will help expand our North American sensibilities:
Global Color Combinations, by Leslie Carbarga (How Design Books, 2001)

To learn more about rich color use, seek these authors:
Making Colors Sing, by Jean Dobie (Watson-Guptill, 1986)
Exploring Color: How to Use and Control Color in Your Painting, by Nita Leland (North Light Books, 1998)

To learn more about applying color:
Color: A Course of Mastering the Art of Mixing Colors, by Betty Edwards (TarcherPerigee, 2004)
The Magical Effects of Color, by Joen Wolfrom, (C&T Publishing, Inc., 2010)

High-brow color learning:
Color Studies, by Edith Anderson Feisner and Ron Reed (Fairchild Books, 2013)

Finding out about ALL things color and how it relates to practically everything:
The Complete Book of Color, by Suzy Chiazzari (Element Books Ltd., 1999)

Color families, moods, and color-planning inspirations:
Pantone Guide to Communicating with Color, by Leatrice Eisemann (HOW Books, 2000)
Color: Messages and Meanings, A Pantone® Color Resource, by Leatrice Eisemann (Hand Books Press, 2006)

Palettes inspired by history:
Pantone: The 20th Century in Color, by Leatrice Eisemann and Keith Recker (Chronicle Books, 2011) Colors are extracted and arrayed in this book with conversation on their history, context, and evolution.

Wanda Kerr's website for growth, artistic expression, and color creativity and her main teaching stream:
www.thewelcomemat.ca

Your Free Trial Of RUG HOOKING MAGAZINE

Join the premier community for rug hookers! Claim your FREE, no-risk issue of *Rug Hooking* Magazine.

Sign up to receive your free trial issue (a $9.95 value).

Love the magazine? Simply pay the invoice for one full year (4 more issues for a total of 5).

Don't love the magazine? No problem! Keep the free issue as our special gift to you, and you owe absolutely nothing!

Get a Free No-Risk Issue

Claim Your FREE Trial Issue Today!

Call us toll-free to subscribe at (877) 297 - 0965
Canadian customers call (866) 375 - 8626
Use PROMO Code: **RHCR917**

- -

Discover inspiration, techniques & patterns in every issue!

Yes! Rush my FREE issue of *Rug Hooking* Magazine and enter my subscription. If I love it, I'll simply pay the invoice for $34.95* for a one year subscription (4 more issues for a total of 5). If I'm not satisfied, I'll return the invoice marked "cancel" and owe absolutely nothing.

SEND NO MONEY NOW-WE'LL BILL YOU LATER

Cut out (or copy) this special coupon and mail to:
Rug Hooking Magazine Subscription Department
PO Box 2263, Williamsport, PA 17703-2263

First Name   Last Name

Postal Address   City   State/Province   Zip/Postal Code

Email Address

* Canadian subscribers add $5/year for S&H + taxes.
Please allow 6-8 weeks for delivery of the first issue.

RHCR917